C0-BNW-363

# Mounting Handicraft

*Ideas and instructions for
assembling and finishing*

## Grete Krøncke

 Van Nostrand Reinhold Company
New York  Cincinnati  Toronto  London  Melbourne

Original Danish edition © Høst and Sons, Publishers,
Copenhagen, 1967
Library of Congress Catalog Card Number 72-123380

Printed and bound in Great Britain by Jarrold and Sons Ltd,
Norwich

Published by Van Nostrand Reinhold Company
A Division of Litton Educational Publishing Inc.
450 West 33rd Street, New York, New York 10001

Published simultaneously in Canada by
Van Nostrand Reinhold, Ltd

1 3 5 7 9 11 13 15 14 12 10 8 6 4 2

Photographs by Jonals Co.

Drawing and diagrams by Grete Petersen

# CONTENTS

# FOREWORD

You have just finished a piece of handiwork. Now what? Some handicrafts can be used almost as they are, while others must have various finishing touches before they can be used.

If you are planning to make gift items, you might just as well face the fact that unless they are completely finished and ready to use it is highly probable that the recipient isn't going to finish them either, and so the gift may even have the opposite effect of what was intended. The recipient develops a guilty conscience, and you will be disappointed when you see your gift is not being used.

One of the reasons for this book is to show that professional-looking finishing techniques are by no means impossible to accomplish or even very difficult. It is mostly a question of knowing exactly how to go about it.

At hospitals, in old-age homes, nursery schools, and other institutions where various handicrafts are taught, usually the leader must guide beginners with the finishing of their projects. For them, this book will be a helpful time saver, and they can use that time advantageously for more personal contact with their students.

This book can be thought of as a supplement to books on occupational therapy and general handicrafts. Don't always follow the instructions too literaly, however, since there are so many possibilities for combining materials, projects, and techniques.

If projects described here appeal to you by all means use the patterns and directions given for them. But that is not the primary purpose of the book. The book is intended to show basic techniques and inspire you to go on by yourself. Once you get the knack of finishing handicrafts, you can adapt ideas from many sources.

There are projects in this book for people within a widely varying range of ability. The author hopes that the easy techniques will encourage the hand worker to try the more difficult ones.

It is especially hoped that this book will help and encourage those who are hesitant about starting a project because they dread the finishing job ahead.

*Grete Krøncke*

# PREPARATION

## Cutting and fitting of materials

Your finished product will be attractive only if the handicraft work is done correctly and with the greatest possible accuracy and care.

Many kinds of material and backing are available for embroidery and stitchery including: monk's cloth (castle erin) (coarse 4 ply has 7 groups of cross-threads to the inch and fine 2 ply has about 13 to the inch); burlap (coarse hessian); linen for crewel embroidery; tapestry canvas (in mesh from coarse $3\frac{1}{2}$ to the inch to 5, 7, 10–12, and 14–15 to the inch); and various waffle-weave fabrics in cotton or other fibers. Check your local needlework departments and mail-order hobby stores for the selections available.

When you plan the craft project, you should calculate how much material you need for the finished project, how large it is going to be, and how large the pattern is going to be. For large patterns, or large repeats, you must also consider where the pattern is to be placed on the project to obtain the best effect.

If you are making a cushion it is a good idea to check into what size cushion forms are readily available. The cushion form should be about $\frac{3}{4}$ inch larger in each direction than the cover in order to fill it out well.

If you are making a handbag or purse, check to see what types and sizes of handles are available, so you can fit the bag you want to make properly.

Some materials shrink when washed. Remember this, especially when you are shopping for table runner, napkin, apron, and rug fabrics. It is also wise to overcast the raw edges of materials you are working on to prevent raveling.

When you are working with a small, repeated pattern, it will not be necessary to figure the pattern placement so exactly. In this case, start the embroidery in the middle of one of the ends and in the middle of a pattern repeat and work out to the sides. In this way the sides will then be equal.

It may be hard to start embroidering if you have no secure way to fasten the thread. Normally, it is a bad idea to start with a knot, since the knot can slip to the right side of the material and you might later stitch into it. Besides, a knot is too bulky. Either let the end of the first thread hang loose and later tack it into the back of the embroidery, or let it remain on the wrong side and stitch over it, to tack it in place. The latter method is suitable for cross-stitch and needlepoint.

You must also tack the end of the thread securely. Do that by sewing it into the wrong side of the embroidery. You must be especially careful with this end-tacking with raffia embroidery because the smooth raffia strands can easily slip out.

Handicraft made by children, patients or elderly people may not always fulfill the general standard requirement of good workmanship. In such cases you may be able to improve the appearance of the items by a careful finishing job.

## Pressing, stiffening, and hemming

When embroidery work is finished, press it and stretch it straight over steam. Put it right side down on a soft, well-padded ironing board and press with a damp cloth placed over the wrong side. In some cases you may have to stretch the embroidery and pin it to the ironing-board pad with stainless steel straight pins before you press it. If you want to avoid getting moisture directly on the embroidery, put a dry cloth underneath a barely damp cloth.

Use iron-on pelon (moycel) or the like to stiffen the piece. Cut corners at right angles and iron with the grain before you sew the project pieces together. Remember to let each piece cool before you continue.

The finish or sizing on a new material may leave a brown film on the bottom of the iron. Remove this film with a soft cloth moistened with vinegar or acetic acid and rub the bottom with paraffin or candle wax, or the film will stain.

Baste the side seams exactly before you sew them. You might even want to use straight pins at points where the pattern lines meet exactly, so they won't shift. When you have sewn the seams, press them open. It is easiest to use a sleeve board for pressing, since you can really get into the corners with it and your pressing therefore has a more professional look about it.

Lining for handbags and purses must be a bit smaller than the outer cover (as opposed to pillows and cushions where the lining must be a bit larger than the cover). Press the edges to be sewn

7

# Preparation

*Sewing the corners. The small scissors show where to cut the material before folding over the corners. Fold corners and press them. Then sew as shown in detail drawing.*

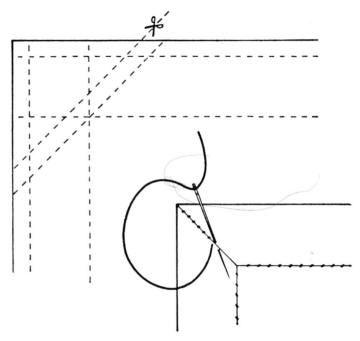

together before sewing them. This makes them easier to sew, and they will look better.

Press corners and hems on tablecloths and napkins before you stitch them. Press slowly as you fold the material. In many cases you can avoid basting if you press the edges first. To avoid scorching the material use a moderate iron. Press down all folds at the corners. It may be necessary to cut some of the extra material and use straight pins before sewing the corner. Sometimes it is a good idea to double the hems on a tablecloth, making the turned-under part the same width as the hem itself. This prevents the turn-under from showing through. On thick materials, however, this will look clumsy, so it is better to make a hem as shown on the drawing.

Edges of napkins and table runners of very heavy material should be finished with a tape or ribbon on the back, in the same color as the fabric.

If you make very narrow hems, sew the corners straight and not at an angle.

# CORDS AND FRINGE FOR FINISHING

For some of the projects illustrated it is necessary to use cords for finishing. Below we show several methods of making cords.


## Weaving spool

Our old, familiar method of spool-weaving is one way of making cords. To refresh your memory, a diagram is given below showing how to do it.

These "horsereins", as they are popularly called, can be used for handles. If you want a soft handle, use the braided cord just as it is formed. One advantage of this cord is that it can be fastened together almost invisibly if you need a circular cord. If you want a strong cord, you can pull a piece of rope or reed through the opening in the cord, as shown.

In many shops you can buy weaving spools ready-made. But they are simple to make from a large empty thread-spool (see drawing). Just hammer in five brads around the hole in the spool.

The procedure is explained in the caption. Children are very enthusiastic about making these "horsereins".

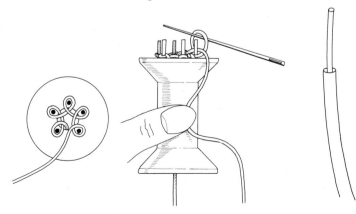

*Make a weaving spool with an empty wooden thread spool. Hammer in five brads around the hole. Pull the yarn through the hole and loop it around the brads as shown. Then wind the yarn around the brads, working from right to left, one stitch at a time. The stitch that is formed around the brad is lifted off, with the aid of a yarn needle, and the new stitch stays on the brad. Continue in this way around the brads, and your woven cord will grow. You can stiffen this kind of cord by running a piece of round reed or stiff cord through it (see diagram at right).*

## Cords and Fringe for Finishing

## Wrapped flag line

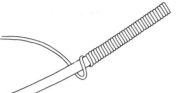

*Wrapped flag line.*

A wrapped flag line produces a solid handle that is easy to make. It can be fastened to the eye screws on a handbag frame by thinning out the last 1½ inch of the line. Put the ends through the eye screws and turn them up so the cord retains a uniform thickness. Secure the ends with a dab of glue and a thin, strong string or thread that you wrap very tightly from the eye screw and up about ¾ inch.

Then wrap the flat line taut—evenly and tightly—with nylon cord, Scandinavian *fiskegarn*, navy cord, or Lily's Double Quick crochet cotton eight-cord cable twist. Wrap back over the beginning material at the eye screw and continue wrapping the entire length of the cord, finishing at the other eye screw. Tuck the ends under with the help of a knitting needle.

## Twisted cord

To make this cord, cut a number of wool strands that will measure together about a quarter of the thickness of the wanted finished strap. Make each strand five to six times as long as the desired length of the finished strap. Collect the threads and loop them around a nail or the like (see diagram). Twist from end B until the yarn feels adequately taut. Now bring end B up to end A keeping it taut all the time and keeping your index finger at the midpoint between A and B. Use your finger to twist the two strands together until they are tight enough. When the cord has been twisted, bind it tightly at the ends.

A

B

A
B

*Twisted cord made from either wool or cotton yarn.*

This cord makes a good border around pillows where the pattern or stripes don't come together neatly. It will divert attention from the mistake. The ends of the cord make decorative tassels.

This is also a suitable cord to use for shoulder bags.

**Knotted or braided cord**

This very useful cord is used for many of the projects given here. It can be braided from several strands of wool, cotton, or raffia. The length of the braiding strands should be eight times as long as the desired length of the finished strap plus about 8 inches.

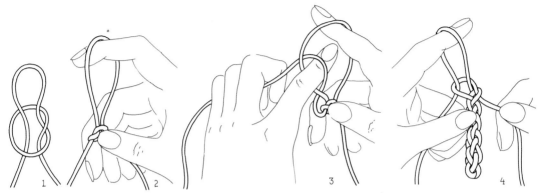

*Knotted or braided cord.*

*Procedure.* Make a loop in the middle of the strand, as though you were starting to cast on stitches in knitting (fig. 1).

Place the loop on your right index finger with the slip-strand at the right (fig. 2). Hold the knot firmly with your right middle finger and thumb.

Catch the left thread with your left index finger from inside the loop and pull it through. This pulls up a new loop (fig. 3).

Now in the same way move the work over to your left hand and pull the loop through with your right hand (fig. 4), then catch the thread with your right index finger, and so on.

Make the cord either loose or tight, depending on the intended use.

**Braided lanyard**

*Lanyard cord.*

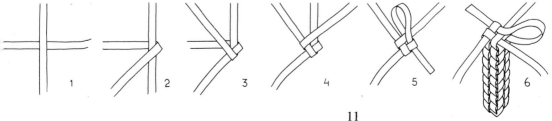

**Cords and Fringe for Finishing**   It is best to use flat materials for this very sturdy strap. Use leather strips, flat shoe laces, or flat plastic strips available at hobby stores.

*Procedure.* Start as in fig. 1 (page 11) and continue following the diagram step by step until fig. 5 is completed. This is the first round. For the next round, begin by bending the last inserted strip backwards. Do the same with the rest of the strands working in order, counter-clockwise.

Do the third round the same as the second, except go clockwise.

Continue by alternating rounds two and three. Fig. 6 shows how the braiding looks after you have done a few rows.

You can use a short strap for a key ring. If you do this, put the key into the first crossover when you start.

## Crocheted cord

This crocheted cord is easy and fast to make once you've learned the knack. The crochet hook should have a pointed end and not be too coarse for the yarn you are using.

*Crocheted cord.*

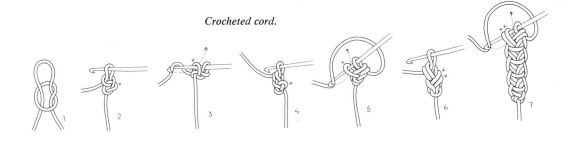

*Procedure.* Make a loop (fig. 1) and chain stitch (fig. 2). Put the hook in through the lower loop (fig. 3) at X and pull it through one loop and then through both of them (fig. 4).

Turn toward the left (fig. 5) and go under the single loop at X on drawing (figs. 4–5) and then through both loops (fig. 6).

Turn the work toward the left (fig. 7) and go under the double loop and through this and then through the two stitches on the crochet hook.

Turn the piece, go under and through the double loop, and continue in this way.

12

## Fringe

A fringe can give your hand work a professional finished look. It is especially pleasing on table runners and place mats, and also makes a nice touch for bags, pillows, rugs, and rya throw rugs.

You can use ready-made fringe for rugs and throw rugs, but in most cases you probably will prefer to make your own.

The photograph shows three types of fringe (more are found on pages 47–51). The two runners in the foreground have fringe made out of the material itself by unraveling the end beyond the cross-stitch pattern. The multicolored fringe in the background is made in a different way. To make this fringe cut the material on grain (along a thread) and hemstitch a suitable distance from the outer edge. Unravel the threads in the material, then knot small bunches of thread (a few strands), in the colors of the embroidery, through the hemstitch hole. In the picture there are four knots of embroidery-thread color followed by four knots of the background material. The threads of the background material lie underneath the tied-on colored threads and the general effect of this is to create a most pleasing pattern.

*On the foreground runners, the fringe is made by unraveling the fabric. The background runner has fringe made by attaching embroidery thread onto a hemstitch row alternately with fringe from the material itself (see text).*

13

# FINISHING PILLOWS
## (cushions)

Pillows are reasonably easy to assemble. The most important thing is to choose a way of finishing the work that harmonizes with the project. The job doesn't take long, but you do have to work with care and accuracy.

### Pressing, measuring, and seaming

When you have finished the embroidery, press it from the wrong side. Use a slightly moist pressing cloth. It is best to have a soft layer or pad underneath while you press to avoid flattening the embroidery.

If the pillow has the design only on the front, start by locating the middle of the embroidery design. Measure out to the desired length and width of the pillow and mark with pins.

If the pillow fabric is big enough to make the back too, fold the material, wrong side out, along the top line. Baste and sew the vertical sides of the pillow and continue around the lower corners, leaving an opening just large enough to insert the pillow form or stuffing.

You can make a corded edge for the pillow from material used for the back of the pillow, from contrasting fabric, or use ready-made braided cord trimming.

*Here is how to turn the corner:*
*1. Put left index finger into corner;*
*2. Fold one seam sharply and hold it firmly;*
*3. Fold the other seam sharply and hold both seams firmly while turning the corner.*
*This way you will achieve a sharp, crisp corner without cutting the fabric.*

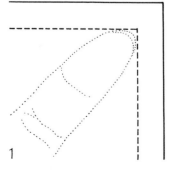
1

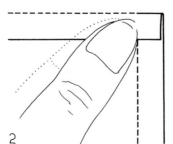
2

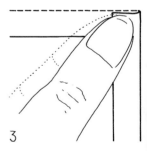
3

The cording piece should be folded double to about ¾ inch. Sew this in place as you would normal cording (see page 17). It makes a nice edge for the pillow. But don't use it on a pillow where the design is continuous (see page 16).

In turning the pillow right side out, be sure to get crisp right-angled corners. Fold first one and then the other seam sharply in each corner and hold them there while you turn that corner (see diagram opposite page). When you do this you get very pretty, clean-cut corners without cutting any of the fabric, which could cause threads to ravel. Do all four corners this way. Insert the pillow form and overcast the opening as shown at right.

## Pillow stuffing or forms

You can make your own stuffed pillow forms, but it is easiest to buy ready-made pillow forms. They are available in several standard sizes, rectangular and circular. Check your local supplier to see what he has, before you begin your project.

Stuffing for pillows is available in kapok, shredded foam, and dacron. Foam and kapok tend to be a bit lumpy. The new dacron stuffing that comes in fluffy layers is the best and most resilient stuffing available.

The pillow must be 1 inch or so larger in each dimension than the cover, or it will not fill out the cover. If it is too small it will look especially bad at the corners. It is far better to choose a pillow form that is too large than one that is too small.

Foam pads or blocks are available for chair or stool covers. Foam rubber is the most expensive and best material, but foam nylon is usable. These come in various thicknesses and sizes. In some places they are available cut to size, in other places they are available only in ready-cut standard dimensions. These should be the same dimension as the cover.

## Two embroidered pillows (cushions)

The two pillows shown in the photograph are embroidered on a loosely woven fabric, such as monk's cloth (castle erin) or a loose waffle weave, using pearl cotton #12 for embroidery.

The pillow on the left uses yellow and white embroidery cotton and black for the dots. It is embroidered on both sides of the pillow, in a continuous design. The pattern matches nicely where the edges are stitched.

Finishing Pillows

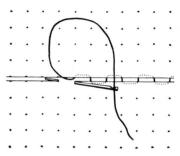

*Sewing a pillow together. After the pillow form has been inserted, sew the opening together with invisible stitches as shown here, alternately from side to side.*

15

The pillow on the right is done with the middle stripe and two outer stripes in white and the other two stripes in yellow. This pillow is finished with a corded edge (see pages 15 and 17).

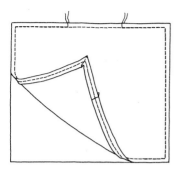

**Corded edge.**

Press a bias tape, cording, or piece of fabric and sew it to the pillow in one piece, all the way around. The closed or folded edge of the band is turned inward, and the raw edges are turned toward the raw outer edge of the pillow. Put the two pillow pieces together and sew the seams. Sew them on the same line as the stitching of the cording. Leave a space for turning the pillow.

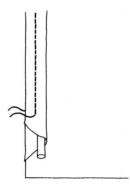

The corded edge can be emphasized if a soft cotton cording is placed inside the bias piece.

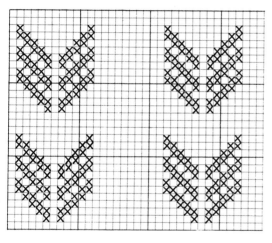

On the left is the pattern for the striped pillow. At the lower left is the pattern for the allover patterned pillow. Lower right is the cushion cover, shown on page 19.

. *white*   X *yellow*   ■ *black*          X *golden brown*   ■ *black*

Finishing Pillows

*Pillow embroidered in heavy wool on coarse jute fabric.*

## Pillow (cushion) of coarse jute cloth

This pillow is embroidered with heavy wool yarn on a very coarse jute fabric (coarse hessian). Use a compatible color and weight for the back of the pillow. The design and stitches are shown in the diagram below. Chain-stitch and outline stitch can also be used on this fabric.

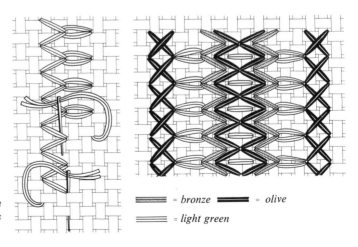

*Left. Some stitches that look good on coarse fabric. Right. These stitches are for the pillow shown above.*

= bronze    = olive

= light green

18

## Cushions

Chair cushions are household items that never go out of style. They

*The cover is cross-stitch in golden brown and black. The back is plain.*

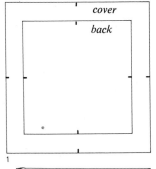

cover

back

1

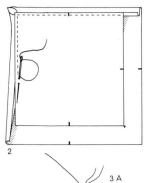

2

3 A

3 B

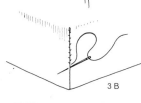

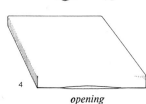

4

opening

are simply too useful. Make them decorative, but be sure to make them harmonize with their surroundings. Cross-stitch is good for indoor cushions. Garden and porch cushions might be better in handprinted fabrics.

MATERIALS:
1 foam block, $17\frac{3}{4}'' \times 17\frac{3}{4}'' \times 2\frac{3}{8}''$.
1 piece of material, $24'' \times 24''$ for cover front.
1 piece of material, $19\frac{1}{4}'' \times 19\frac{1}{4}''$ for cover back.

As a rule, you should purchase a piece of foam exactly the size you want to use for the cushion.

Cut the two pieces of material from the same fabric, if you want the cushion to be the same front and back.

*Procedure*: The front of the cover must be large enough to stretch down over the $2\frac{3}{8}$-inch sides of the foam block. To figure the size of your fabric cover, you must add the thickness of the foam block to each side, or $17\frac{3}{4}$ inches plus $4\frac{3}{4}$ inches, and add two seams, each $\frac{3}{4}$ inch or total of $1\frac{1}{2}$ inch. The material will then measure $24 \times 24$ inches. That is what you should cut ($17\frac{3}{4}+4\frac{3}{4}+1\frac{1}{2}$ inches).

The back of the cushion cover should measure $17\frac{3}{4}$ inches plus room for two seams, each $\frac{3}{4}$ inch, or $19\frac{1}{4}$ inches for each side, after cutting.

*Finishing*. The most important steps in the finishing work are illustrated in the drawings on this page. Start by marking both pieces of material at the middle of the edges on all four sides (fig. 1). On the front cover mark all four corners with a dot. These dots show where the corners of the nylon block will come.

Fig. 2 shows how the pieces of material are put together, right sides facing each other. Put straight pins in at the four marking points and baste the pieces together from corner to corner. Sew the seams on the machine. The corners will stand out like cones because of the extra material. Leave an opening on one side large enough to insert the nylon foam block (fig. 4).

Fig. 3 shows two different methods of making the corners. A shows how to sew the corner from corner dot to corner of the back piece. Figure $\frac{3}{4}$ inch for the seam allowance and cut off the rest. B shows how to sew the corner from the outside after you have inserted the block. Cut off some of the material and turn it in from the mark at the top down to the corner of the back piece and overcast together as close to invisibly as possible.

When you insert the foam block, position the seams as inconspicuously as possible. Finish the opening of the cushion with invisible stitches (see page 15).

20

Finishing Pillows

*Portable stool cushion. The zipper is placed opposite the handle. You can even slip a newspaper or book inside the cushion if you're taking it to the park or the like.*

## Pillow (cushion) with handle

This pillow is handy to carry around with you to sporting events, on picnics, and the like. It will make the hardest bench or stool feel comfortable.

MATERIALS:
1 foam block, $15'' \times 16\frac{1}{2}'' \times 1\frac{1}{2}''$.
1 piece of material, $17\frac{3}{4}'' \times 35\frac{1}{2}''$ for cover.
1 zipper 8–12".

*Procedure.* The important thing here is to choose a material that can take use both indoors and outdoors. The zipper makes it possible to remove and wash the cover easily. You can decorate the cover with embroidery or textile printing.

21

### Finishing Pillows

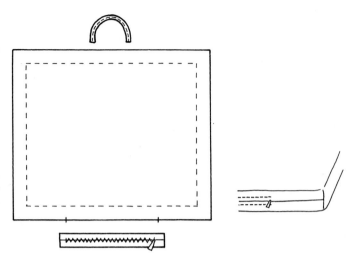

*The measurements of the pillow fabric must correspond to the measurement of the foam block, plus its thickness and seam allowance. The corners can be made by pushing the fabric back inside and sewing at the corner with invisible stitches.*

Make the handle from a narrow strip of the material or a tape doubled several times. A suitable length is 6 inches. Lay the cover material double with the wrong sides up. Insert the strap in the middle of the long side. The ends will be in the seam and the curve should turn inward, between the two layers of the material.

Sew by machine all the way around. The finished measurements of the cover should be about $15\frac{3}{4} \times 17\frac{1}{4}$ inches. On the side opposite the strap, leave an opening for the zipper (see diagram).

Finish the corners to fit the nylon block as described on page 20.

### Pillow (cushion) with an edge

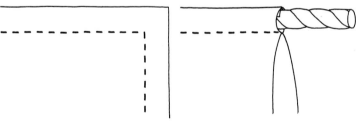

A SMALL FINISHING TIP. After sewing the pillow together (right sides facing), turn the pillow and along the edge, about $\frac{3}{8}$ inch in, sew small tacking stitches all the way around so that a decorative edging forms. If you want to make a more pronounced edge, place a thick, soft cording inside and sew along it, as shown in the diagram.

22

# HANDBAGS AND PURSES

The easiest part of making a handbag or purse is embroidering or creating the design. Then comes the finishing. Finishing really makes the difference in the appearance of the handbag, so it should be done smartly, exactly, and carefully. It pays to spend time on finishing your handbag whether it is an everyday bag or a dressy little purse.

The photographs in this section show several models and many ideas for finishing them. The descriptions are short, but they should be sufficient for you to carry on the work by yourself. In addition, the preface of this book includes many helpful hints and general instructions that you should read before making your handbag.

### Stiffening (handbags)

When you finish the cover and press it, you are often faced with the problem: "Should I stiffen this bag? Is it too limp?"

If the bag is just slightly limp, you can stiffen it with a lining. But often this is not enough. You can get a better job with iron-on pelon (moycel) interfacing.

Iron on the pelon (moycel) before you sew the embroidered pieces together. Cut it to size so that the corners are at right angles and iron it on the back of the embroidery, exactly on the grain. In certain cases it might be best to iron it on the lining material, such as when the body is made of raffia or Swistraw (raffine), or monk's cloth (castle erin) embroidered with those materials. You cannot use iron-on pelon (moycel) on these because of the raffia or Swistraw (raffine) strands that are also on the back of the material.

For handbags that should stand up, such as those with chain handles, it is necessary to use two thicknesses of iron-on pelon (moycel).

Iron with a very hot iron, but not so hot that it scorches. Let the work cool before you continue with it.

In some cases, such as textile-printed fabrics, you can stiffen the bags with a thin layer of foam rubber cut without a seam allowance, so it reaches exactly from side seam to side seam. Make it a little bit shorter than the bag, so that it clears the top seams.

Starched burlap (coarse hessian) is also useful for stiffening, such as for knit handbags (see page 25). It is even better if you can find double-starched burlap (coarse hessian). Many weights of horsehair canvas or buckram are also available in fabric shops.

Where only slight stiffening is required, such as for fabric bags a stiff cotton duck can be used.

If the bag is to be very stiff, a cardboard that is pliable but firm can be used.

Synthetic parchment, mainly used for lampshades, is also a possibility in some cases.

## Side seams and corners

When the side seams have been sewn, press them open. Whether you will sew the side seams all the way up depends on the shape and type of handle mounting you are using. Sometimes you must leave a slit so the folding handle mechanism can be accommodated. In any case, match the pattern at the seams.

Thickening the corners of a bag can be done in two ways. You can take the corners in from the inside (see diagram) or you can push them in from the outside and sew them down invisibly. Striped handbags look best if you push in the corners so that one of the stripes continues all the way around.

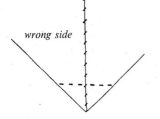

*wrong side*

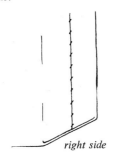

*right side*

*Top shows corners sewn from the inside, and the bottom shows the corners tucked in and sewn from the outside.*

## Lining handbags

A good handbag should have inside pockets. On one side you can make a little pocket for keys, change, etc. The pocket can be set in flat, or it can have a gathered elastic top. Take care of the extra material at the bottom of the pocket by making pleats.

Larger and deeper pockets for special purposes, such as long narrow ones for pens, pencils, or eyeglass cases, can also be made.

You can include a zippered pocket. The easiest way to make these is to use the new magic zippers called "Hook N' Loop", (Velcro) for example, which is really two nylon bands that adhere when pressed together. One of these bands is fitted with a large number of small tempered-nylon hooks and the other has the same number of loops. A slight touch locks the two together. A slight pull opens it. Just sew the strips in place.

24

## Handbags and Purses

*This tote bag was knitted in Indian colors—brown, gold, and natural. A circular needle was used. Bag and handle are lined.*

*handle*

## Knitted tote bag

It was hard to find a proper finishing technique for this bag, but we finally succeeded. The method is so good that we have used it for many other handbags and purses as well, including raffia bags.

This tote must be stiff enough to stand by itself. That means that it is absolutely necessary to use a stiff insert, such as double-starched burlap (coarse hessian) or two layers of iron-on pelon (moycel). Stiffen the bottom with stiff cardboard or a similar material with a smooth, shiny surface.

□ - *white*
| - *ochre*
× - *brown*  →

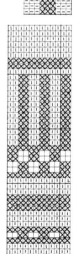

*Pattern for the knitted tote. Arrow indicates middle of bag.*

25

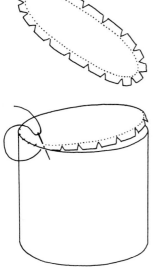

*Procedure.* Knit according to pattern. For woven and embroidered bags make a cardboard bottom as shown in the drawing. Cut the cardboard and fasten it to the bottom of the bag, before you sew it in place.

Make the handle firm with stiffening material and line it before attaching.

Cut the lining a bit smaller than the outer material. This is also true for the bottom lining.

Sew the lining pieces together. Sew in the lining bottom. The piece will be sack-shaped. Insert. Be sure that it fills the bag out and lies smooth.

Press seams of the lining before inserting. Sew lining to the top of the bag with invisible stitches a little down from the edge.

Make the bottom this way: bind off the knitting except for a piece that corresponds to the front of the bag. From here knit a straight piece as long as the bag sides are wide. Now bind off. Sew the bottom piece to the other sides. Cut the cardboard pieces and put them in place.

*Here's how to make the bottom of the tote bag. The bag was made in one piece, with a bottom piece included.*

## Two shoulder bags

Both shoulder bags in the picture opposite measure about 9 by 9 inches. The size can be changed. Other materials and designs can be used.

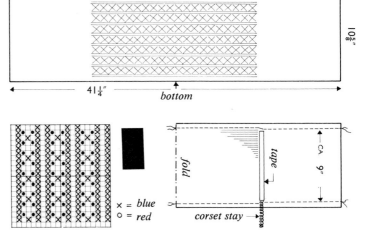

*Top: placement of the embroidery on the fabric. At right; stiffening a bag with a corset stay. At left: pattern for embroidered shoulder bag.*

26

## Self-lined embroidered bag

MATERIALS:

1 piece coarse monk's cloth (castle erin, coarse hessian), $10\frac{5}{8}'' \times 41\frac{1}{4}''$.
Red and blue pearl cotton #8. Same colors for cord.
1 corset stay, about 9″.

*Procedure.* Overcast the raw edges. Lay the large pieces double and measure 10 inches from the fold (which later forms the bottom) in both directions. Sew basting stitches here (see diagrams on page 26).

Now do the embroidery in a long stripe pattern from one basting thread to the other.

27

Sew a tape at the end of the embroidery, so that a corset stay can be inserted through it. This keeps the top edge of the bag firm.

Press the piece on the wrong side and lay it double, right side together. Sew along both sides. As shown in the diagram on page 26 the unembroidered part measures a little smaller than the embroidery. This becomes the lining.

Turn the piece and press the unseamed bottom edges toward the wrong side and stitch together with invisible stitches. Press along the top edge of the embroidery. If you prefer to have a colored lining in the bag, you can add one. Otherwise this makes a self-lined bag.

Make a twisted cord of cotton yarn stretched between two chairs (see page 10).

Carefully bind the ends of the finished cord, about 2 inches from the ends. Pin the cord in position and sew it to the outside side seams of the bag. The ends of the cord make pretty tassels. Trim them.

### The crocheted bag

This bag uses eighteen crocheted squares. Each square is about $3\frac{1}{8} \times 3\frac{1}{8}$ inches. Use two harmonizing colors, possibly light and dark shades of the same color. Leftover yarn is good for this project.

Sew the squares together, three in one direction and six in the other. Sew the side seams. Attach cord. Insert a lining.

### Embroidered striped handbags

*Bag shown in foreground, opposite.* This has homemade handles, You can make them any size you like.

*Materials:*
1 piece monk's cloth (castle erin), $13\frac{3}{4}'' \times 25\frac{1}{2}''$.
2 pieces monk's cloth (castle erin), $3\frac{1}{8}'' \times 10''$.
1 piece lining, $13\frac{3}{4}'' \times 25\frac{1}{2}''$.
Pearl cotton #8, dark blue and medium blue.
2 dowel rods, $\frac{3}{8}''$ thick and $8\frac{1}{4}''$ long.
4 eye screws.
1 braided or knotted cord.

Procedure. The measurements given in the list of materials are easy enough to change if you want a larger or smaller bag.

Before you begin the finishing, get the dowel rods cut to size, so you can make the casings at the top of the bag the right size to fit them.

The diagrams on the following page illustrate this step-by-step procedure:

1. Sew the large piece together at the sides, all the way to the top. Use the small pieces for the dowel casings. Turn the ends in and sew them in place.

2. Fix the corners. One of the stripes should follow the seam all the way round.

3. Lay the two pieces double with right sides out and sew on top. Make sure the dowel will fit before you sew.

4. Press the top edge down all the way around.

5. Drill holes for eye screws in dowel ends and screw them in. Use

*The handbag on the right is embroidered in stripes. It has an inexpensive but effective fastening mechanism made from dowel rods and eye screws. A knotted cord is used for the handles. If you pull both loops you have an ordinary length handle, if you pull only one, you have a shoulder-bag handle.*

*The bag at the left, standing, is made from a handwoven Hungarian table napkin. The handle is the same as described on page 30.*

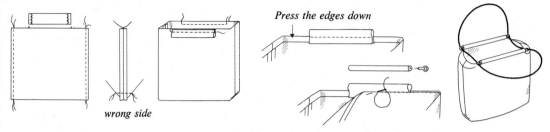

*Press the edges down*

*wrong side*

*Details of the procedure described in the text for making dowel rod closing.*

a drill thinner than the screw itself for pre-drilling the holes and make sure the wood doesn't split.

6. Stitch the lining in place at top.

7. Braid, crochet, or knot cord (see pages 9–11).

8. Put cord through the holes of eye screws. Join the ends as inconspicuously as possible to form a ring.

If the bag doesn't drape properly at the top, press in a couple of sharp folds with a lukewarm iron. The bag should close by itself when you pull on both sides of the cord.

You can stiffen the bottom of the bag with a piece of cardboard with rounded edges, if desired.

### Woven striped bag

The striped, woven bag shown opposite is finished in the same way except the handle is made of two knotted straps.

Weave the material $11\frac{7}{8}$ inches wide. Weaving yarn leftovers will make fine material for the cord. Sew the bag material together.

### Woven plain bag

The bag on the left, opposite, is woven in one long piece and fringed at the ends. It is sewn together at the sides.

*Procedure.* Sew the side seams together. Don't forget to turn the top fringed flap to the outside (see diagram, page 32).

Cut the dowel rods. Calculate the length so that the bag has a sufficiently large opening on the top.

Drill a small hole at the ends of the dowel rods. The hole should be smaller than the size of the eye screw you will screw into them. It is easiest to drill these holes if you fasten the dowel rods in a vise.

Position the top flaps and insert the dowels under them. Stitch in place (see diagram). Make a little hole in the outer fabric through

which you can put the eye screws into the small holes at the ends of the dowel rods.

Sew the corners at the bottom and cut out two pieces of thin cardboard or pasteboard. Put one piece down in the bottom and under the corner points. Insert four paper fasteners from the right side so they go through the material and the cardboard. Spread out the prongs as shown in the diagram, page 32. Cover the other piece of cardboard with material and fasten it with glue. Sew it on the inside bottom of the bag. This effectively covers the prongs of the paper fasteners. The knobs form little feet on the outside bottom of the bag.

Make the cord of yarn in a compatible color (see pages 9–11). Sew the ends together as inconspicuously as possible.

Finish the upright bag pictured on page 29 in the same way. This, incidentally, was once a handwoven Hungarian table napkin. Now it's a delightful handbag.

*Left. The handle is made from a cord run through four eye screws. It is an inexpensive but effective closing. Right. The bag has two separate cord handles, but otherwise the method is the same.*

31

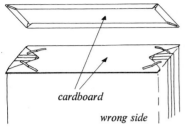

cardboard

wrong side

*Attach the stiffened cardboard bottom securely with four paper fasteners from beneath. Hide the prongs with a piece of cloth-covered cardboard glued or sewn on.*

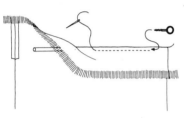

*Sew in the dowel rods at the top edge of the bag.*

## Raffia handbag with flap

The raffia handbag shown opposite measures $9\frac{1}{2}$ inches wide by $8\frac{3}{4}$ inches high. Sew it on tapestry canvas and cut it in one piece (see diagram, top page 34). You can use other materials, but in that case, cut the bag according to the lower pattern on page 34.

MATERIALS:

1 piece tapestry canvas, $15'' \times 24\frac{3}{4}''$.
Swistraw (raffine) in several colors.
1 piece lining, $13\frac{3}{4}'' \times 23\frac{5}{8}''$.
1 dowel, approximately $9\frac{1}{2}''$ long.
2 eye screws.
$15\frac{3}{4}''$ flag line for handle.
Wrapping twine or cord for flag line.

*Procedure.* When you have embroidered the bag, press it with a moist cloth and stretch it over steam, if necessary.

Sew the bag together at the sides. If it has been sewn on tapestry canvas, sew the two side seams together and sew in the corners. If you use other materials you must sew the two side pieces in separately, as shown in the diagram on page 34.

Cut the dowel to suitable length ($9\frac{1}{2}$ inches on this model). Drill holes for the eye screws. Position these holes about $1\frac{1}{2}$ inch in from the ends and $6\frac{1}{2}$ inches apart.

Sew the dowel inside the flap, using strong yarn or buttonhole thread. Stitches should be as close to invisible as possible, and as tight as possible.

The lining should be somewhat smaller than the outer fabric. Sew it together and fasten it in place along the edge of the flap in the same way as you would fasten it to an open top. Make stitches as nearly invisible as possible. Press down the edges first; this makes it easier to sew.

Make the button for the closure from two different-size rings sewn together, as shown in the diagram on page 33. Sew it on the flap by stitching around the inner ring. Make a large loop, cover it with buttonhole stitches, and attach it to the bag. The loop and button form the closing for this bag.

Work the eye screws cautiously through the fabric and into the pre-drilled holes of the dowel rods. Locate the holes with a needle first. A dab of glue on the threads of the screw will hold it in place. But be careful not to get glue on the material.

Make the bag handle from flag line about 16 inches long. Unravel the ends and thin them down a little. Put them through the

32

*This raffia bag was made by an older woman. She chose the colors and created the design herself.*

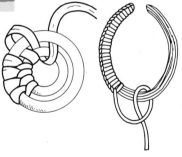

*Button and loop for closing the bag.*

33

*Pattern for raffia bag. Use the top pattern for tapestry canvas. Use the lower pattern with the separate side pieces for other materials.*

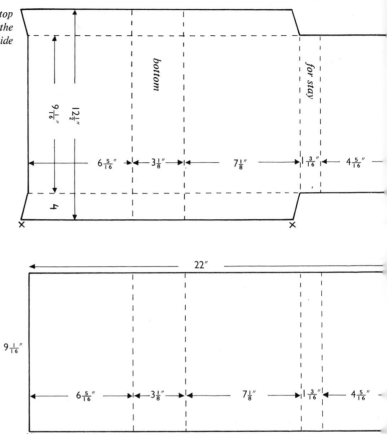

eyes, bend them back, and fasten around the line with strong thread and a dab of glue. (See also pages 9–11.)

The drawing shows how to wrap the handle. You can use colored *fiskegarn*, navy cord, or Lily's "Double Quick" crochet cotton eight-cord cable twist. Wrap evenly, tightly, closely. Fasten the ends well.

More suggestions for making handles appear on pages 46 and 47.

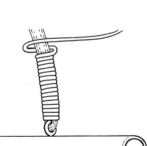

*The handle is wrapped flag line.*

34

## Bags with chain handles

Here are two different ways to finish chain-handled bags:
TYPE 1. This bag is very wide and roomy. It is most useful, but perhaps it is not as elegant as the others.

MATERIALS:
Fabric (see below).
Lining, same size as fabric.
2 pieces of iron-on pelon (moycel), same size as lining.
1 chain handle.

*Procedure.* You can decide how high you want your bag. Then calculate the width of the material by opening the handle mechanism and measuring half of its circumference, along the opening. This will give you the width.

*Bag with chain handle (type 1). The simpler the lock you use, the more the embroidery shows up.*

35

Handbags and Purses ASSEMBLY INSTRUCTIONS:

1. Press the embroidery. Iron on the two pieces of pelon (moycel). Let it cool.

2. Fold the material at the middle, right sides together. Baste the side seams and sew them up completely. Make sure that the circumference of the bag material corresponds exactly with the circumference of the handle opening. If this is not the case, correct the mistake now. While sewing the sides together, make sure that the pattern on the sides is symmetrical.

3. Press side seams open and sew down the corners on both sides (see diagram below).

4. Cut the lining and sew. It must be a bit smaller than the outer material.

5. Press the top edge down. It must follow the pattern of the embroidery to look well.

6. Sew a narrow tape on top to make a casing for the rod. The tape should be about ⅜ inch shorter than the rod, and the distance from the top edge should be about the same as the distance between the lower edge of the lock and the rod. The opening marked with an X on the diagram will then be covered by the material.

7. Turn the bag right side out.

8. Push the rods through the material and behind the tape. You can

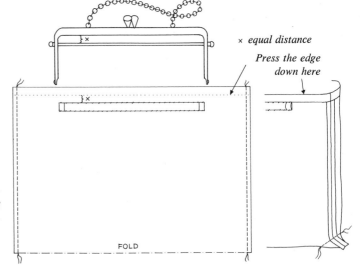

Diagram shows how to sew the bag and where to position the tape used to make a casing for the detachable brass rod of the handle mechanism. Note also how to treat the bottom corner of the bag.

use a knitting needle to open up the material when you insert the rod. Put the rods through the eyelets of the handle and check that everything is in good order, height and width. Then take out the rods.

9. Stitch the lining to the top with invisible stitches.

10. Re-insert the rods through the eyelets of the handle. Apply cellulose glue (Duco cement) or nail polish on the threads before you screw on the knobs.

11. Open the lock completely. Tack the side seams with strong thread to the lowest part of the handle.

When you close the bag it has a delightfully chubby shape, which we can't quite reproduce in the photograph. If you prefer it with sharp folds, you can make them by using an iron.

Finally, one little remark on the technique of embroidering: If you embroider according to a ready-purchased pattern, remember that flowers should be mirror images on the two sides. The easiest way to get them right is to start at the middle of the bottom and work your way up in either direction. Then you won't get your flowers upside down on one side.

TYPE 2: Assembly of these bags can hardly be called a job for beginners. You should be able to do a satisfactory job, however, if you follow the instructions carefully.

MATERIALS:
1 8″ chain handle with detachable rod.
1 piece embroidered material, $19\frac{3}{4}″$ and $2\frac{3}{8}″$ wider than the handle, plus seams (see below).
1 piece of lining $11\frac{7}{8}″ \times 19\frac{3}{4}″$.
2 pieces iron-on pelon (moycel), $11\frac{7}{8}″ \times 19\frac{3}{4}″$.

*Procedure.* Since the material, especially the leno-weave, may pull together somewhat during the sewing, you should cut it larger than desired, for example, $13\frac{3}{4} \times 21\frac{5}{8}$ inches. Do the final fitting as you do the assembling of the pieces.

Press the embroidery on the wrong side. Cut the pelon (moycel) with right-angle corners and iron it on the material along the grain.

Leave a slit in the side seams. Baste and sew the seams only as far up as needed, leaving the opening corresponding to the size of the lower, hinged part of the frame.

Then follow the directions for Type 1 bag from step 3 to step 8, and again from step 10.

*These two chain-handle bags have side slits (type 2). Left. This one is stitched on leno fabric with fiske-garn or navy cord. Right. This is embroidered in pearl cotton on coarse, loosely woven fabric like monk's cloth (castle erin).*

Sew in the lining with invisible stitches along the upper edge. Put in the extra material at the slit so that the edge forms a diagonal line down to its bottom. If it is too bulky even after pressing, you can trim off some of the excess material, but do it cautiously!

Finally sew on the lining a little down from the top edge. Press. Put in the rods as described and put a dab of glue or nail polish on the screw threads before you screw them into the knobs. Tack the bottom of the slit and the lower part of the frame together with strong thread. Push the top edge under the frame of the handle.

38

## Two casual bags

The photograph on page 41 shows two casual bags, one with a wooden closing and one made with burlap (coarse hessian), using a decorative hemstitching and with a cord handle. They are rather rough in appearance but very attractive nonetheless.

### BAG WITH WOODEN CLOSING

Make the handles the size you want them. It's not hard to do if you can locate the right size molding.

MATERIALS:
1 piece dark blue monk's cloth (castle erin), $13\frac{3}{4}'' \times 21\frac{5}{8}''$.
1 piece lining, $13\frac{3}{4}'' \times 21\frac{5}{8}''$.
1 piece iron-on pelon (moycel), $27\frac{1}{2}'' \times 43\frac{1}{4}''$.
Pearl cotton #8 in medium and light blue.
1 piece rabbeted wood molding, $19\frac{3}{4}'' \times \frac{3}{4}'' \times \frac{1}{4}''$ thick (see illustration). Use teak or some other good wood.

*Procedure.* Overcast the raw edges and start the embroidery in a corner about $\frac{3}{4}$ inch from the edges. Sew seven squares across the width and fifteen squares along the length (see the pattern drawing above).

Stitch the two side pieces on your fabric a little bit away from the main piece. They should be one square wide by five squares long. Stitch another one of these a little further down on the material. Leave about $1\frac{1}{2}$ inch space between your pieces.

Press the embroidery on the wrong side. Cut the pelon (moycel) into two pieces with right-angled corners. Iron them on with the grain.

Attach the bag side pieces from the wrong side. First sew the bottoms of your side pieces to the middle row of the bag, or row 8. Then sew the sides (see photograph on page 41). Use the stitch shown on the diagram on page 40 for attaching the pieces invisibly. This will blend right into the pattern and you will not need to make the cross-stitches along the sides as you are embroidering the main pieces. You will be doing the cross-stitch row when you attach the pieces.

Cut the wooden molding piece with a saw, making it the exact length of the width of the bag at the top. Cut both molding pieces the same length. Be sure to saw at sharp right angles, not on a slant.

Drill two holes in the notched part of the molding with a $\frac{1}{32}$-inch drill bit. The holes must be parallel and be spaced equally.

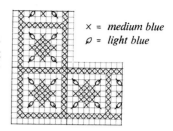

x = *medium blue*
ø = *light blue*

*Pattern for the embroidered bag on page 38.*

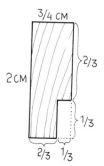

*This is a section view of the wooden molding used as a handbag handle. Rabbeted moldings are not always available in stock at lumber companies, but they can be made to order. It is possible to use a molding without the rabbet for this purse handle. Note: numbers are proportions, if not marked as inches.*

3/4 CM

2/3

2 CM

1/3

2/3  1/3

39

## Handbags and Purses

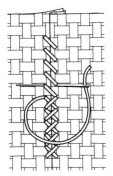

*Attach pieces with cross-stitches so that the seam blends into the pattern completely.*

*Sew the outer fabric through the holes drilled in the rabbeted wooden molding piece.*

*Sew on the lining through the same holes as the outer fabric, but on the other side.*

Place them about ⅛ inch from the inner edge of the notch (see diagram). The outer hole should be about ⅛ inch from the ends.

Drill four holes in each piece of molding for the handle cords, in pairs at each end as shown in the diagram.

After drilling the holes, sand the molding pieces with fine sandpaper and treat them with teak oil (Scanoil) (Rustin's) or lacquer. Use a surface treatment that suits the wood you have selected.

Four little wooden knobs are made for securing the ends of the handle cord (see diagram on page 42). It is easiest to drill the holes in these knobs before you saw them out of a piece of wood. You can drill holes in pre-cut knobs if you place the drill in a vise, pressing the knobs down on it while turning the drill handle, but you have to watch out for your fingers. It is an awkward way to do it. Your handmade knobs can be shaped by sanding and rounding the sharp edges.

*Attaching handles.* Put the right side of the embroidery against the side of the handle that has the notch (see diagram). Sew through the holes, as shown. Tighten stitches well, using a strong thread such as button or carpet thread. With this method, the outer material will lie level with the upper part of the handle.

Leave a slit open on one side of the lining. Then you can turn it back for stitching in place. The lining should have the same shape as the bag, but make it a little bit smaller. Put the right side of the lining against the smooth side of the handle and sew through the holes (see diagram). When you have sewn both sides, turn the lining over the outer material and put it into the inside of the bag. Sew the slit together.

Knot a cord (see pages 10–11) in a suitable length and in a color matching the bag. Cotton or wool yarn work well for this. If the holes for the cord are too small, you can enlarge them by working

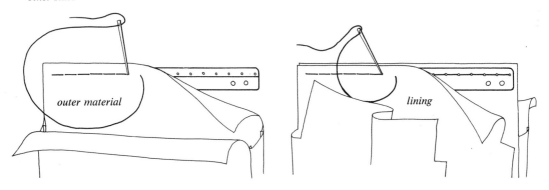

outer material

lining

a round file or piece of rolled sandpaper in and out of the holes.
Insert the cords through the holes as shown on the diagram.
Attach the wooden knobs. The two cords should not be equally
long, because one is positioned further in on the molding than the
other. But cut your cord pieces to adjust for this, so that when the
bag is closed, the handles will be of equal length.

*The hand-made handles for these two handbags go nicely with their casual appearance. Left. Teak-wood molding is mounted at the top of the bag. The cord is held in place by four small teak knobs. Right. The knotted strap is inserted through large covered rings. The upper edge is kept straight by means of a corset stay.*

BURLAP (COARSE HESSIAN) HANDBAG

The bag shown on the right in the photograph on page 41 is made of burlap.

MATERIALS:
1 piece of gold-color burlap (coarse hessian), $10'' \times 24\frac{3}{8}''$.
3 corset stays, each $8\frac{3}{4}''$ long.
2 large rings.
1 piece tape or ribbon, $19\frac{3}{4}''$ long.
Woolen yarn, same color as burlap (coarse hessian).

*This shows how the bag closing works. Notice the wooden knobs at the ends of the cord.*

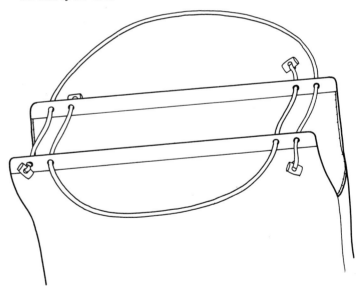

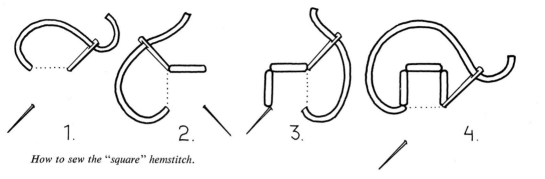

1.    2.    3.    4.

*How to sew the "square" hemstitch.*

*Pull out five threads (about 1¾ to 2 inches in from outer edge) adjacent to the outer row of hemstitch. Turn back flap as described in text and sew second row of hemstitch through both layers of fabric.*

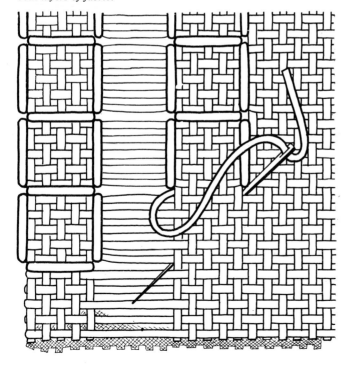

**Handbags and Purses**

*Procedure.* Pull out five threads in the burlap (coarse hessian), about 1¾ inch in from each narrow end. Sew the outside row of square hemstitching (see diagram page 43). Fold the flap down into place, and sew the inner row of hemstitching through the two thicknesses of the fabric.

Lay the material double, with the right sides facing, and sew the side seams from the bottom fold up to the notched place on the drawing. This is the place where the flap is folded back. Turn the material to the right side, and hand-stitch the flap pieces together. Press seams open.

Following the diagram, sew on, by hand, a narrow tape or ribbon on the wrong side of the purse. This will form a casing for the corset stay. It must fit the length exactly. If it is too long, break it off to fit, and bind the end with tape. Also put a corset stay on each side of the bag, inside.

Cover the two rings with buttonhole stitches. Sew them in the corners of the bag top.

Make a cord from woolen yarn the same color as the burlap (coarse hessian) of the bag (see pages 9–11). Pull the cord through the rings and sew the ends together as inconspicuously as possible.

If you pull on only one of the cord loops, it will be long enough to use as a shoulder bag. If you pull on both loops, the handle will be ordinary length.

*Cutting pattern for burlap handbag. Notice how the corset stay is inserted into a tape canal made by hand-stitching a tape in place as shown.*

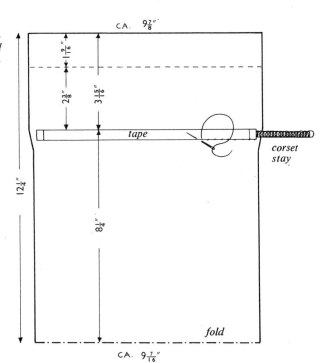

### HANDBAG WITH WOODEN HANDLES

Wooden handles can be purchased in hobby stores and knitting shops. These handbags are best if they have side insert pieces as shown in the drawings. This one has a cardboard bottom and is quite stiff.

Attach the lining to the top of the bag, a bit down from the edge, along the dotted line shown on the drawing.

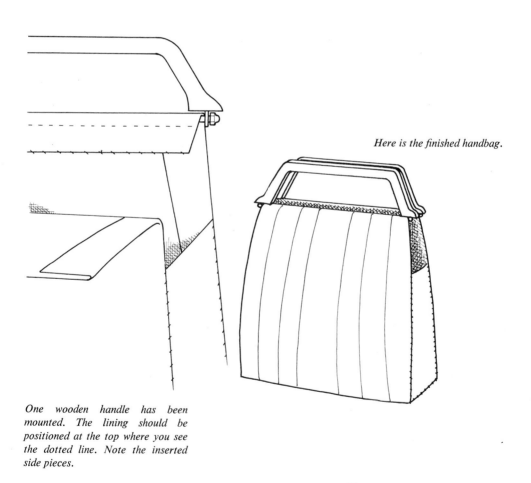

*Here is the finished handbag.*

*One wooden handle has been mounted. The lining should be positioned at the top where you see the dotted line. Note the inserted side pieces.*

BAGS WITH CORD AND RING HANDLES

Sew the bag using one piece of fabric, $13 \times 25\frac{1}{2}$ inches plus seam allowances. Cut the lining the same size as the outer material.

Lay the designed (embroidered) sides together and sew the side seams. Sew in the corners so the bottom will be half as wide as it is long.

Divide the top edge into three equal parts and sew rings at these marks. Insert the cord through the rings as shown and secure them at the side seams.

*A simple but effective closing. Notice that the handle cord is tacked to the side seams at the top so that they pull inward when you carry the bag.*

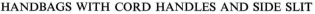

*The closing here uses two flat wooden molding pieces with holes, sewn under the fabric. Note the side slits, needed to get down into the bag.*

## HANDBAGS WITH CORD HANDLES AND SIDE SLIT

Insert narrow wooden strips in the top edge of the purse. Holes should be pre-drilled in the wooden strips before inserting them. Reinforce the material at the holes with either buttonhole stitches, eyelets, or leather rings glued on.

The side pieces can be straight across the top, or they may have slits. The latter is best for bags with narrow bottoms, because the slits make the opening wider.

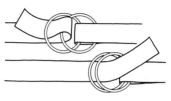

Handbag made from handwoven fabric. Insert a corset stay at the top for support. The cord is twisted as described on page 10.

Below. Fringe is twisted as shown. Take four threads, twist them in twos, both in the same direction. Twist the resulting two together but in the opposite direction. Knot ends.

Place the two rings on a piece of cord and attach it to bag flap. The other loose cord is pulled through the rings to fasten the bag. It is anchored at the bottom of the bag.

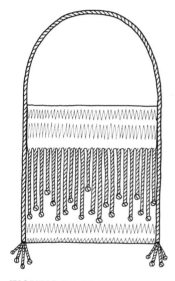

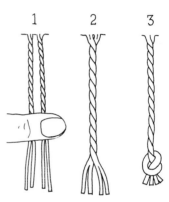

## WOVEN BAGS WITH FRINGE

Weave the material on a 12-inch loom. Use a striped pattern. Weave the piece two and a half times as long as the desired bag height. The warp must be figured long enough to allow for the hanging twisted fringe as shown on the diagram. The fringe must be twisted by twos before knotting. You can add beads to this fringe before you make the knots for a dressy effect.

Make the cord of weaving yarn in a suitable thickness (see page 10). Decide for yourself whether the handle is to be long or short.

## THREE VARIATIONS

These three bags are meant to supplement the raffia bag design on page 33. The shape is the same, but the handle and fastener are different.

1. Insert a dowel rod at the top as was done for the raffia bag, but screw the eye screws into the ends of the dowel. The cord handle is attached to them.

Bag 1. Simple but very pretty handle. Closing is made with two rings.

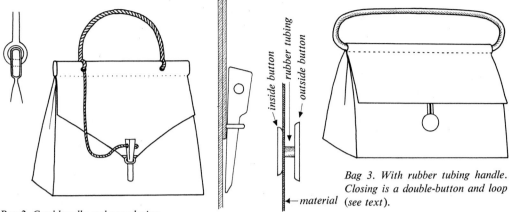

Bag 2. Cord handle and peg closing.

Bag 3. With rubber tubing handle. Closing is a double-button and loop material (see text).

2. On this model you use a flat stick instead of the round dowel rod. Two holes are drilled in it for the cord handle. The cord for the fastener. also goes through one of these holes. The fastener is made by shaping a peg and drilling a hole in it through which the cord is inserted. A ring for the peg is attached to the bag.

3. Make this handle of rubber tubing. The closing consists of a leather loop sewn into the hem of the flap and a button on the bag. Place a small cylinder of rubber tubing around the shank of the button and anchor it with a small button on the back (see diagram). This is a good technique for fasteners and buttons that will get a lot of hard use. It prevents the fabric from tearing.

SHOULDER BAGS

These are easy to make. Just take one long piece of cloth, laid double. Sew up each side completely. Fold the top over to make a flap. Use a corset stay for support at the fold. You get into the bag through the flap opening. It is really just a bag with its mouth folded over!

They can be made of leather or other rather stiff material. It can have a long or a short handle (see pages 9–11).

BAGS WITH FRINGE

This bag is also made of one long piece of cloth. Embroider both ends as shown in the bottom diagram. The unembroidered part forms the lining of the bag. The embroidery should be slightly narrower than the width of the cloth, as the diagrams clearly show.

Shoulder bag with long cord. The flap at the top is stiffened with a corset stay.

48

Follow the dotted lines. The normal seam allowance for the embroidered part is $\frac{5}{8}$ inch.

Sew along the top edge of the bag with long looped stitches going through the fold line, as shown on the drawing of the finished bag. This is done after the lining section has been pushed down inside the bag, and the top fold line pressed in place.

Attach the two outside pieces along the bottom, but leave the fringe hanging so it can be knotted. Take two threads from each side and knot them together to form the fringe.

Insert the bag handle before you close the bottom, so you can fasten it inside the lining. A corset stay may also be put in the bottom before it is stitched closed and the fringe drawn together.

## DOUBLE BAG WITH FRINGE

The procedure for making this bag is shown in the diagrams. One long piece of material forms the inside of the pockets and has a looped portion that fits over the rod of the handle. In addition

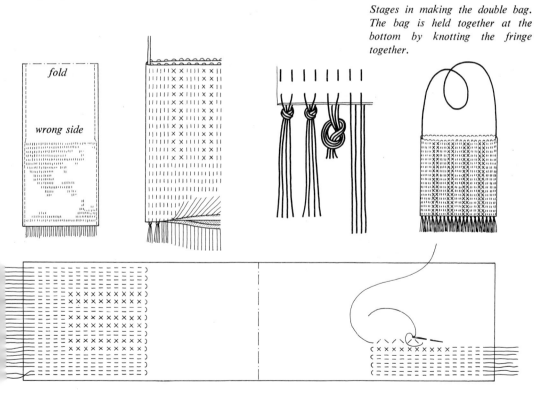

Stages in making the double bag. The bag is held together at the bottom by knotting the fringe together.

there are two embroidered pieces for the outsides of the pockets, and one longer piece (about 22 inches) that forms the back of the pockets and middle of bag.

Fringe the ends of the 22-inch piece and the embroidered pocket pieces. Knot the fringe. Sew the pieces together as shown in the diagram.

Insert a metal rod or dowel through the looped portion. If you use a metal rod there should be a way of attaching eyelet loops to the ends for attaching the handle cord. Eye screws and a dowel rod work fine. If you use a ready-made handle with detachable rods, make the bag to fit the rod size.

*At the right is the cutting pattern and below the method of folding and sewing this bag.*

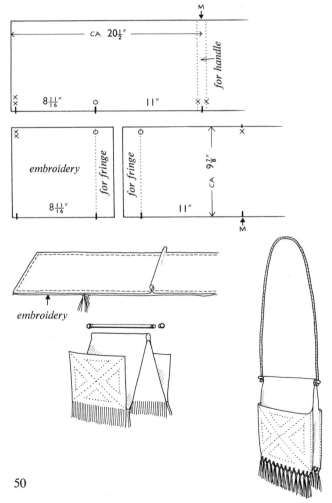

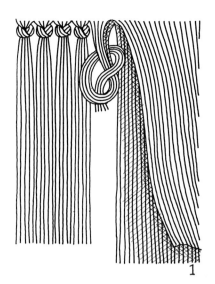

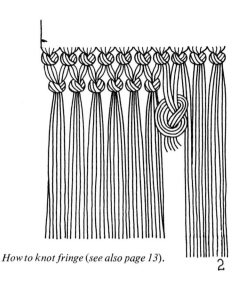

*How to knot fringe (see also page 13).*

1

2

## DOUBLE HANDBAG WITHOUT FRINGE

This bag is like the one previously described. Finish it completely and then sew on the embroidered decoration to the pocket flaps.

You have a lot of leeway in decorating this bag. You can fringe all four edges of the pocket flap piece or make some other amusing edge.

The bag is made from two pieces 40 inches long. It is hard to get

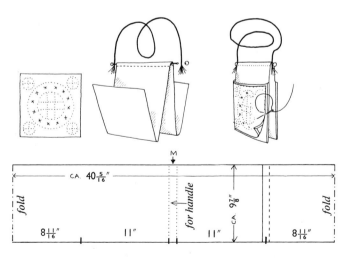

On this double-pocketed bag sew on the embroidered flaps after finishing the bag. The lower drawing shows the simple cutting pattern.

51

such long pieces, but you can sew pieces together, sewing them at the bottom of the pockets.

In this instance, make the loop opening through both layers of cloth, or only on one layer, as done with the other double bag.

### FASTENING IDEAS

The raffia bag on page 33 has a hand-made fastener. Here are some more suggestions. A bamboo piece makes a smart fastener. Cut it at the joints, using a hack saw. Drill a hole through the middle. Sew through this hole to attach the bamboo to the purse.

The fastener on the right is made by using a package-carrying handle, such as department stores sometimes fasten to your shoe- and dress-box cords to make them easier to carry. In both cases attach the fastener to the bag so there is space to loop the cord around the ends as shown in the drawing.

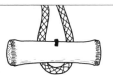
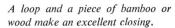

*A loop and a piece of bamboo or wood make an excellent closing.*

# MAKING LAMPSHADES

Lampshades can be expensive and difficult to find in just the right color and shape for the room you are decorating, therefore many people have started making their own lampshades. This is one way to get what you want!

You can decide on size, shape, color, and design. Your lampshade will have some character instead of being lifeless and sad-looking as so many of them are. Of course, it is also possible to make lampshades with more "character" than beauty.

One should really have an entire book on this topic. We are not able to go into great depth here. Our main objective is to show how to make and finish a few basic types of hand-made lampshades.

## Two fabric lampshades

MATERIALS: (for the two shades at left in the photograph on page 55.)
1 lampshade frame.
Fabric for covering frame (embroidered or handprinted).
Elastic.
Ribbon or tape.

*Procedure.* To determine the size for your lampshade material, measure the largest circumference of the lampshade frame (in this case the lower frame). Add a seam allowance. Measure the height of the frame, preferably along a perpendicular rod. Place the rod next to the middle hole on the top ring and about $3\frac{1}{8}$ inches in from the lower ring. Measure this distance and add seam allowances at top and bottom. If the shade is to have a gathered ruffle on the top, add on enough material for it before you cut.

The middle shade shown in the photograph is the simplest possible kind to make. Sew the cover material together at the sides. Make a $\frac{3}{8}$-inch hem casing for the elastic at the top and bottom of the shade. Draw the elastic and pull the cover from the top down over frame. Arrange evenly and neatly and secure ends of the elastic.

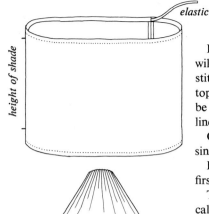

elastic

*An elastic is inserted in the casing at the top and bottom of the lampshade. Pull it taut around the frame. You may use tape for the upper elastic if you need to tighten it more.*

If this shade is going to have a top ruffle, as in the left shade, you will have to make the casing for the elastic by sewing two rows of stitching about ⅜ inch apart and an appropriate distance from the top. You make an extra large hem at the top so that the ruffle will be double thickness, and the gathering casing will be at the hemline.

Often a piece of ribbon or tape is used for this instead of elastic, since it is possible to pull the material more tightly together.

In sewing the casing seams, fold them double and press them first, before machine-stitching.

The handprinted fabric for the lampshade at right was made by calculating the exact space between the upper and lower rims of the frame, dividing this into equal rows, and block-printing the design.

## A paper shade

Next time you are ready to throw out an old paper lampshade, be sure to save the frame. It could be used again!

The frame at the right in the photograph opposite consists of a couple of rings, joined by vertical shafts, and a rim that fits the socket housing. Such simple frames are often used on factory made shades.

Sometimes the paper is glued to the rims, but as a rule it is better to sew it on through holes punched along the edges.

Remove the old paper carefully and spread it out on a table. Measure to see how much you need for a new covering.

There are many suitable materials that can be used. We used synthetic parchment here, because it is easy to work with and doesn't fade from use.

If you are lucky enough to remove the old paper shade without damaging it, the easiest way to make a pattern for the new shade is to trace around the old shade. You can simply lay it down on the fresh parchment and draw the pattern with a soft pencil. Mark the holes, too, then you won't have to guess at them later.

Cut the parchment following your lines. Make the holes with a paper punch.

If the old frame has very worn rims, smooth them with sandpaper and paint them with an alkyd paint (enamelling paint) before attaching the new shade.

Fastening and decorating this shade are described on pages 92–93.

54

The two shades at left are very easy
to make. They are also very easy to
remove from the frame when you
want to wash the fabric. The shade at
right is made by re-using an old
frame. The decoration is dried,
pressed flowers. For flower-pressing
directions see page 93.

**Three cylindrical shades**

The shades shown at the left and right in the photograph opposite are inexpensive to make. But you can give them your own special touch in the selection of material and decorative treatment. For example:

*Creative stitchery* and embroidery (the only problem with these is that the tacked ends and threads on the wrong side will cast a shadow.

*Pressed flowers* on the parchment.

*Handprinted* fabrics.

*Appliqué.*

*Drawings* (possibly your children's drawings).

*Procedure.* Place the lampshade-covering material on a table, wrong side up. Cut only after gluing the parchment layer to the decorative layer. Use hobby glue (plastic glue with clear transparent bond such as Elmer's glue (Bostik, Evostik).

Turn the piece over and see if the covering material is smooth and evenly attached to the parchment. If so, press the layers together, gently. When the glue is bone dry cut the piece to shape.

Make holes through the glued layers at the ends where the shade will be sewn together. Use a paper punch or revolving punch with a small diameter. For sharp, clean holes, place a piece of cardboard or thick paper over the fabric. Cut through both edges of the lampshade at the same time holding them in place with paper clips or clothes pins.

RAFFIA-WEAVE SHADE at the left in the photograph is self-supporting. It doesn't need a frame. The top is decorated with a stitching of natural raffia. This is partly for decoration and partly to make the top edge even. Glue the parchment on the inside and let it extend to about an inch from the bottom edge of the material. Then, when the glue has dried, ravel the edges of the raffia weave back to the edge of the parchment.

You can make a pattern in the shade itself by pulling threads from the raffia weave in a decorative pattern. Or you might purchase raffia mats already made in pattern weave.

Four thin wooden sticks are used to support the shade. Insert them in pairs across the shade, making a cross that fits over the lamp socket. Make the holes about ⅜ inch from the edge, and be sure the holes are centered exactly, or the shade will hang crookedly.

56

*The shades at the left and right do not need frames. The fabric is glued to synthetic parchment and shaped in a cylinder. The middle shade is made on a frame. The design is "square" hemstitching.*

57

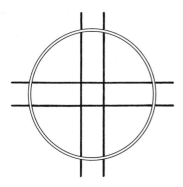

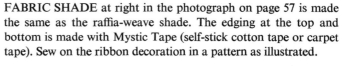

*Make the lamp support by inserting four thin sticks to form a double cross at the center.*

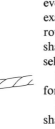

*Wrap the rings of the lamp frame in this way with lacing.*

FABRIC SHADE at right in the photograph on page 57 is made the same as the raffia-weave shade. The edging at the top and bottom is made with Mystic Tape (self-stick cotton tape or carpet tape). Sew on the ribbon decoration in a pattern as illustrated.

CYLINDRICAL SHADE at top center of the photograph on page 57 is made over a frame.

MATERIALS:
1 cylindrical frame.
Lacing.
Embroidery thread.
Linen fabric.

*Procedure.* Wrap the top and bottom rings of the frame with lacing, evenly and tightly (see diagram). The linen fabric must fit the frame exactly, without drawing up. Sew square hemstitch in perpendicular rows at positions just outside the upright frame rods. Sew the shade piece together at the last row of hemstitching, using a selvage edge and making the joint as inconspicuous as possible.

If you like you can do some decorative stitchery in the panels formed by the hemstitching.

Make a row of hemstitching along the top and bottom of the shade. Turn edges and make another row of hemstitching through both layers (see diagram on page 43). Calculate the height of the shade exactly so that the material will sit tightly on the frame.

Sew the lining together so that its circumference is about ¾ inch smaller than the circumference of the ring of the frame (using a taut outside measure). Place the lining inside the frame and sew it to the upper and lower rings through holes in the hemstitching and around the rings.

## Bottle lamp with raffia shade

You may not realize it, but this lamp is made from a fifth of whisky —the bottle, that is. (Vat 69 and Seagram's Benchmark have this shape. D.O.M. or B & B liqueur bottles can be substituted, but they do not have the footed base.) The empty flask makes an unusual and shapely lamp base.

It is covered with small mosaic tiles available by the sheet in hobby stores. The tile comes in various sizes and colors and is fine for this purpose. The tile looks natural since it is in matte finish

58

The lamp base is a whisky bottle covered with mosaic tile. The shade is made of raffia weave. You'll have to glue a layer of thin fabric to the bottle before you can attach the tiles.

59

and approximates the color of natural stones. And this mosaic tile is easy to work with.

*Procedure.* When the bottle is empty, wash it and dry it carefully. Drill a hole for cord first (see page 61). Cover the bottle with thin fabric smeared with hobby glue to make it stick to the glass surface. The material must sit evenly, tightly, and smoothly.

Now you can glue on the mosaic tile. This can be done by gluing on a whole sheet at a time around the cylindrical part of the bottle, but you will get better results if you sort out the tiles and glue them on one at a time. Save the smaller ones for the conical neck of the bottle where you need to vary the spacing and positioning of the tiles to make them fit properly.

Start the tiles just above the foot of the bottle. Glue them so they are equidistant—that is maintain the same size joints as they did when they were on the sheet. Apply the glue to the surface of your bottle a little bit at a time. You can get a special glue or tile grout for the mosaic tiles, but ordinary hobby glue can be used.

When you have attached all the tiles, let the whole project dry for twenty-four hours.

Now you have to put in the joints. Use a special cement or grout for this, which you can buy when you purchase the tiles. Press the grout well down between the tiles, and when the space is filled remove the excess with a moist cloth or sponge. At the bottom, even out the grout to make the footed edge of the bottle stand out clearly as an accent.

The grout will be white when you buy it, and this looks unsuitable with the raffia shade and mosaic colors. You can tint your grout as you make it up by using a little of the ordinary instant coffee (not the freeze-dried).

If you happen to use the white grout, you might still be able to tint the grout by using a soft, colored paper napkin that bleeds when wet. But you must do this while the grout is partly moist. Just rub the napkin along the joints and some of the color will come off. However, this method is not very reliable. It is best to tint the grout with powdered pigment when you are mixing it.

### Socket and cord for lamp mounting

The mounting is made by using a stopper, knurled nut, and threaded pipe, as shown below. The socket is screwed into this. This makes a sturdy lamp-socket holder.

It is necessary to make a hole in the bottle, near the base, so the lamp cord can be run out of the bottle. This makes a neat-looking job and solves the problem of a dangling cord.

If you have a hand drill or a slow-speed variable speed electric drill, or a twist drill with a hardened carbide tip, you can drill the hole yourself.

If you have never drilled on glass before, practise first on some bottles you do not intend to use for a project!

Scratch a cross mark with a file or steel nail on the glass where you want to drill the ⅜-inch hole. It is impossible to drill on smooth glass surfaces, so the cross mark is needed to give the drill a place to bite. Don't press too hard on the drill nor angle it. Hold the bottle securely. It is best to fasten it between a couple of padded boards. Foam rubber, or other padding, will serve the purpose.

The drill will work better if it is lubricated with turpentine or kerosene (paraffin). You can build a little dam of putty or clay around the drill hole to keep the drops of lubricant from running off.

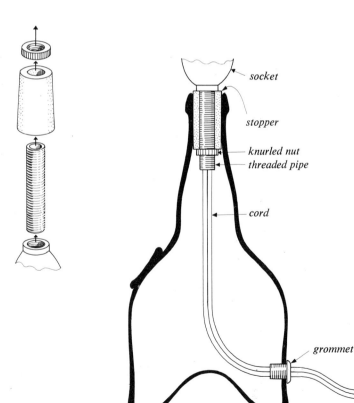

socket

stopper

knurled nut
threaded pipe

cord

grommet

*This is the method for mounting the lamp cord and socket. You will have to have a hole drilled in the bottom of the bottle for the cord.*

If you don't feel equal to drilling on glass, take it to a glazier and let him do it.

Insert a threaded grommet into the hole you have drilled. The lip on the grommet will be on the outside of the bottle and may be glued in place with epoxy cement.

Run the cord through the grommet and fish it up through the neck of the bottle. Use a hook made of bent wire to catch the cord. Mount the lamp socket on the threaded brass pipe, which has been inserted in the stopper, and tighten it into the socket with the knurled nut. You may want to glue the stopper to the pipe if it is not a snug fit. Use a dab of glue and be sure the socket is straight before the glue dries.

This method makes a good lamp mounting. It takes a shade with a squeeze clip that fits over the lamp bulb. If you do not want this kind of shade, or if your shade is not equipped with these clips, you may want to use the so-called harp socket, which has a wire structure that flares out around the bulb and ends in a top that screws into an opening in the inner top rim of the shade.

If you are not handy with electrical wiring and the like, you may want to have an electrician or handyman friend do this job for you.


### Raffia lampshade

MATERIALS:
A clip-shade frame, tall enough so that the lower edge will cover the socket and the upper neck of the bottle.
Raffia woven fabric or even a place mat of raffia might work. Burlap is also possible.
Lining.
Lacing.
Colored raffia strands.

*Procedure.* The outer material should be the same height and width as the frame plus seam allowances.

When you have overcast the raw edges, pull out the threads and make the decorative border as shown in the drawing. Sew the vertical seams so that the material fits the lower ring exactly. Press seams open.

Sew the lining together. It should have a circumference ¾ inch smaller than the ring.

Wrap the frame rings with lacing.

*Pattern for embroidery design on raffia shade.*

Turn the edges of the lining and sew it to the laced frame. Make sure that it is smooth at the bottom and pleated at the top.

For the bottom of the shade, calculate the seam allowance as $\frac{5}{8}$ or $\frac{3}{4}$ inch. Turn half of this back and baste in place. Pull the embroidered material over the frame and then turn back the rest of the seam allowance and sew it to the lining with very small stitches and a very strong thread. (Sew through the outer layer of material without letting the stitches show.)

Run a basting stitch around the top of the material. Tighten it to fit the ring. Sew the material to the ring with a strong thread. Clip off any excess material when you have finished.

Cover a round cardboard disc, cut to fit the top ring, with the material and sew this covered disc as invisibly as possible to the top of the ring over the gathered material. You may want to glue the material to the cardboard with hobby glue.

# BOOK COVERS

### Guest book cover

A guest book is an excellent housewarming gift, and with your hand-made cover it becomes a very personal gift.

The guest book in the photograph opposite is decorated with cross-stitch design, but you can use other embroidery or creative stitchery techniques.

Buy the book first. Then decide on the embroidery and design appropriate to the size of the book and the taste of the intended receiver.

Choose a book covered in white opaque material, or cover your book with white material first, so the book itself won't show through your cover.

Attach the lining material with hobby glue or white book-binding glue. Cut the book loose carefully with a sharp knife at the head band at the top and bottom (see the very dark line on the diagram), and fold the glued material edges over the book boards and push it in under the back. Use a dull knife to help press it under the spine.

Fold the corners as shown in the diagram on page 70. When the glue is dry, reinforce the groove between the spine and the cover boards with tape.

The embroidered cover should be made long enough to provide for a large pocket at each end. The covers of the book are inserted into these pockets. Exactly at the center, where the spine of the book will be, you should reinforce the embroidered material with a ribbon tape on the inside.

Press the embroidery and lay it with right sides together. Tack the two large pockets at the ends. Tack one at the top only. Make a trial fit and correct any problems. The cover should fit snugly, but not so tight that it cramps the spine or stretches the embroidery.

After this trial, sew the pocket seams on the inside. Be sure to end the flaps a little bit away from the spine, or you won't be able to close the book completely.

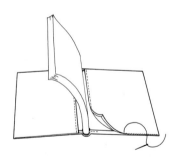

*Note the way the covering fabric is turned over and pushed under the spine of the book. This is only done when the original cover is apt to shine through the embroidered cover and a lining cover is needed.*

*Sew this edge of the pocket flap last and by hand.*

*Let your imagination go when you design your guest book! This needle-point pattern came from Peru.*

*The large book at the right is a ring binder for recipes and clippings. The spine design is textile printing. The front design is a kind of fabric painting over a rough surface. The book cover at the left is an adjustable model. It can be moved from book to book. A bookmark in the same design can be seen in the book.*

After sewing three of the seams, turn the material to the right side, fit it on the book and sew the last seam by hand, as seen in the diagram.

To protect the embroidery from dirt, use Scotchguard spray.

It is best to wash the material before you make the cover, so it won't shrink in later washings. You can also stiffen the material with a thin gelatine solution, which makes it more dirt resistant as well. (One package ($\frac{1}{2}$ oz.) of gelatin to 1–2 quarts of water.)

### Two book covers

Handprinted fabrics and raffia embroidery work make attractive book covers and you can let your imagination go when creating your own design.

This is a large ring notebook for recipes or clippings. We used unbleached muslin for the cover and large pockets for inserting the book.

Use the same procedure as described for the guest book, page 64. The handprinted decoration on the spine is made with two block designs. One is used for the middle design, the other is used for the top and bottom design. We used the same motif for the lampshade on page 55.

The front and back decoration of this book cover is made in an unconventional way. Spread the material out taut on a slab of cement or other very rough surface, such as a wood-wool (cement) slab. Dip a broad, flat brush into textile paint. Rub off the excess and run the brush over the material, using long, rapid strokes. The color will "take" only where the raised surface touches the material.

If you can't find a wood-wool slab, use a piece of corrugated cardboard. And if you turn the cardboard 90 degrees after painting once, you can get a plaid effect if you go over it again.

Various materials might be used for the underlay in making such designs. Use your imagination and experiment on scraps, before doing the final project.

## Little Book Cover

This is not a permanent cover for one book. You can shift it from book to book. The design here is a textile print using a sea-horse pattern. It will usually be necessary to stiffen the fabric with a layer of iron-on pelon (moycel) interfacing. This could be covered with a lining, hemmed in place.

Make the book cover in one long piece. The length of this piece is about 22 inches. Make a pocket on the wrong side at one end, about $3\frac{1}{8}$ inches deep. Simply fold the material back and sew along the edges.

Don't make a pocket at the other end. Stick the book cover into the one flap, and fold the other flap inside the front of the book. Then, as you read, you can use the adjustable front flap as a book-mark.

This type of book cover can be used on thick and thin books. Make it in a standard $8\frac{1}{2}$ or 9-inch, height to fit most fiction books. You could also make one in a size to fit paperback books.

Book Covers　**Bookmark**

Look back at the photograph of the two book covers. In the smaller book we have placed a bookmark that matches the cover design. For this one we used a fabric that had one color warp and another color weft, so when we raveled the edges they were different colors, giving an attractive effect.

This material also makes good handprinted Christmas cards. Solid white material is also effective.

Glue the material to a card of smooth bristol board; or even 3 by 5-inch index cards will work. They are cheaper, too.

**Telephone notepad**

MATERIALS
Burlap (coarse hessian) or raffia weave.
Swistraw (Raffine) in brown color.
Swistraw (Raffine) in green for cat's eyes.
A notepad with cardboard back.
Pencil.
Heavy cardboard (possibly bookbinders' cloth) and glue.

*Procedure.* Make the edging design by sewing raffia strands in an over-and-under stitch through the loose weave. You actually follow one of the warp or weft threads and pull in your raffia on top of it. The cat design is made in petit point, as shown in the drawing.

The front cover piece (with the design on it) should be made large enough to fit the pad, with a seam allowance to allow it to be wrapped over the cardboard stiffener, and should be long enough to cover the entire front, top spine, and go a little way down the back, where it will be met and covered by the back cover piece (see diagram on page 70).

Sew the embroidery and press it. Glue the embroidered cover to the cardboard stiffener for the top, and the smaller stiffener for the top spine, as shown in the illustration. Don't use too much glue. Sometimes all that is needed is just a layer of glue on the edges that turn over the cardboard. If you use burlap (coarse hessian), it is best to apply a thick layer of glue to the cardboard and the burlap (coarse hessian). Arrange the corners as shown in the diagram.

The back part of the pad cover should have two layers of cardboard attached to the fabric, one piece shorter than the other, to form a pocket into which the notepad slips. So don't glue them together all around. Leave a slot for the notepad.

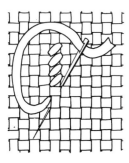

*Petit point stitches: sew under two threads for each stitch.*

68

## Book Covers

The telephone notepad is made of burlap (*coarse hessian*) *or raffia weave and the cat design is stitched with Swistraw* (*Raffine*).

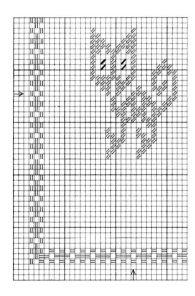

|| // - *rust*
/ - *green*

*Pattern for cat design.*

69

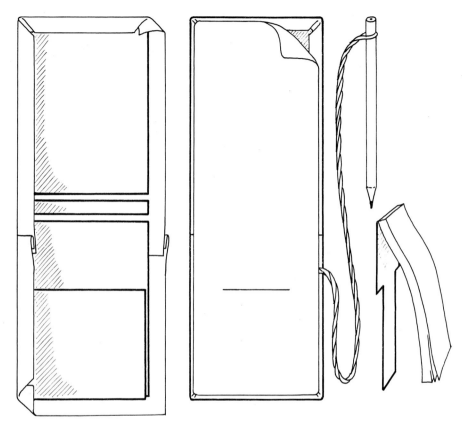

*Stages in making telephone notepad. Notice the extra piece of cardboard and the slit in the lining piece. The back of the pad is cut in a T shape to fit into the holder.*

Bristol board makes a good stiffener for this project. Book-binders' cloth might be used for the back cover piece. Cut a lining piece of lightweight bristol board, shaping it to fit as shown in the diagram. It is smaller than the outside cover. Before gluing it in place, take a decorative string or cord and attach it to the pencil. Ravel the other end and flatten it out. Glue between the two layers of the notepad cover.

Cut a T-shaped flap out of the back of the notepad cardboard, as in the diagram, and insert this into the small slot you have cut in the lining cardboard. Mark the position of this slot and cut it before gluing the piece in place.

This same technique can be used for covering a block of letter paper. You could even cover a box as a holder for envelopes to go along with it.

70

# COVERED BOXES

Covered boxes are handy for storing many things: jewelry, stockings, sewing gear, handkerchiefs, letters, writing supplies, and the like. And you can decorate these boxes with almost any kind of handicraft techniques from embroidery to textile printing.

The coverings shown in the photograph on page 73 are embroidered. The embroidery work is rather easy, but covering the box might cause some trouble. It has to be done very exactly if the box is going to look workman like when it is finished.

You can make your own boxes from cardboard and cover them with fabric, stitching the fabric at the corners. This is a very time-consuming job, and if you forget to allow for the thickness of the cardboard and fabric, the box will be crooked. The method shown here is much easier, but it still requires exacting work and patience.

The principle here is to build two boxes in one, one inside the other, and the only visible sewing will be along the top edge.

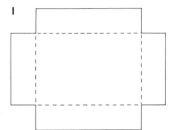

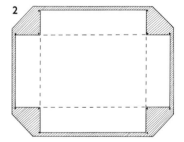

*Procedure.* Mark the box shape in the desired size on chipboard or bristol board (fig. 1). With a sharp knife, cut along the solid line and scratch a scoring line along the dotted line (don't cut these through).

Carefully bend the side pieces downward along the scored lines. Flatten out the board again and put it on top of the material you are going to cover it with (fig. 2).

Cut the material, allowing for seam allowances, and clip corners off diagonally. At each corner put three marks as shown in fig. 2.

Sew the corners on the machine following your marks (fig. 3).

Turn the material with the sewn corners inward. Insert the box into the material and pull the corners into the inside of the box (fig. 4).

When this is done you must examine the work carefully to see if it is tight enough. If you are using thick material it might be necessary to cut off some of the board in the corners. When you are sure that the corner seams sit right, glue the triangular corner

*Rectangular boxes are easiest to make in the double-box method. The outside box and the inside box are each covered, then they are glued together. Note the corners, especially.*

71

**Covered Boxes** pieces to the box. Smear glue on the edge of the fabric that turns over the box sides, and press it down (fig. 4). The glue (white hobby glue) is then applied to the bristol board surface.

Make the inside of the box in the same way, but if you want to you can make it from thinner cardboard. It should be just enough smaller to fit down into the first box you made, after this has been covered. When you cover the inside box, however, you pull the corner triangles to the *outside* of the box and glue them there (fig. 5).

When you have finished the inside box, put it into the outer one and sew the two together with invisible stitches (fig. 6).

It's easy to make the boxes, but it can be somewhat difficult to fit them accurately. It is impossible to give exact measurements, since the board and fabric vary so much. Trial and error is the only system here.

You can make a pretty lid for this double-box. The lid is made of two pieces of cardboard cut to fit the box. The top piece is covered with an embroidered fabric, while the inside should match the rest of the box covering. These two pieces are stitched together by hand after you have positioned them on the cardboard. The hinged edge is made by sewing the flap to the back of the box.

The little rectangular box shown is made with a lid that has an embroidered doily sewn to the top fabric. If you want a soft lid, you can insert a thin foam layer for padding under the embroidered top.

The little round box is the kind some fancy imported cheeses come in. The fabric is glued to the box with a little overlap along the top edge. This is turned down inside and covered with the lining material.

The bottom overlap must be clipped to make it lie smoothly. Glue it in place. The lining is paper glued in place.

Make the cover in two parts. Make a circular fabric disc a little larger than the cover of the box, and make an edge piece. Cover the edge with a straight piece of fabric, turned over the top and bottom. Cover the top with the circular disc fabric. You may want

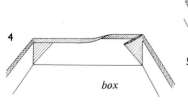

4

box

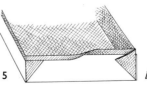

5

lining

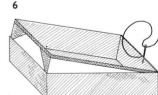

6

*The rectangular boxes are hand-made. We used the clever method described in the text. Decoration for the small box is described in the text. The round box is an imported cheese box.*

*Two matchboxes and a bridge scorepad, covered with embroidered or textile-printed fabrics.*

74

to slip a lining of foam rubber under it to make the top soft and puffy. Sew the two parts of the lid together with cross-stitches along the rims. Line the inside with paper, glued on, to match the lining of the box.

## Matchboxes

Matchboxes may be covered with textile-printed fabrics or embroidered pieces. Glue the decorated fabric to a piece of cardboard that is slightly larger than the top of a large matchbox. You want a small overhang all the way around. Make the corners as shown on page 71. (Note that the embroidered example here was made to fit the matchbox top exactly, without an overhang.)

Make a bottom piece for the matchbox to match the top, but without the design. That way you can tell if you've got the box right side up.

## Matchbox with mosaic tiles

Follow the same technique for covering the box as is used for the lamp described on page 60, using leftover tiles from the lamp project. Before starting to glue on the tiles, lacquer the case with clear lacquer to protect it against moisture from the glue.

## Bridge scorepad

This is made in the same manner as described for the telephone note pad.

# TEA COSY

There's nothing like a pretty tea cosy to keep your teapot, or coffee pot, warm until you're ready for that second cup. Any of your handicraft embroideries or textile printings will be handsomely displayed in this manner. The method of assembly below is a quick and easy one.

MATERIALS:

1 piece of foam rubber, $12\frac{5}{8}'' \times 23\frac{5}{8} \times \frac{3}{4}''$.
1 piece cotton fabric, $15\frac{3}{4}'' \times 53''$, to cover foam rubber.
1 piece outer cover (see below).

*Procedure.* First hem each of the short ends of the piece of cotton that will cover the foam rubber. Then fold these ends back with right sides together so that they meet at the center, with one flap overlapping the other. The folded piece should be $23\frac{5}{8}$ inches long as shown on the diagram. The width should be $12\frac{5}{8}$ inches. Sew side seams. Turn the material right side out and press. Insert the foam piece in the lining and make sure it fills out the corners. Now you can tack the four corners together.

*Cover.* The cover on the model is made of embroidered loosely woven fabric. The pattern is shown at the right. The cover piece should be cut $15\frac{3}{4} \times 25\frac{5}{8}$ inches. The first dimension is the width of the tea cosy.

When the embroidery is finished, press it on the wrong side. Fold material together, right sides together, and sew side seams. Fold the top corners in so they fit the inner foam padding. Corners are done the same as for handbag bottoms as shown on page 24. Hem the bottom. Slip cover over liner. One of the great advantages of this tea cosy is that it all comes apart for washing.

76

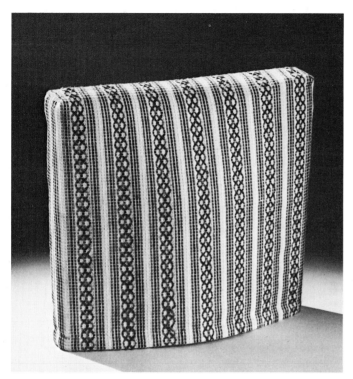

You can't make an easier tea cosy!
This is an embroidered cover and a
loose inner stuffing. That's all.

Lining pattern for form stuffing.
Procedure is described in the text.

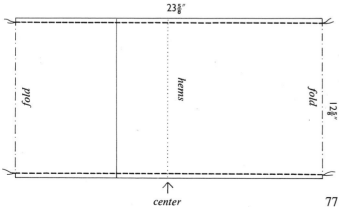

23⅝″

fold

hems

fold

12⅝″

↑
center

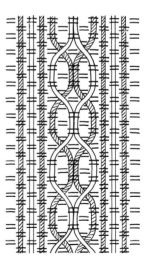

Here unbleached linen is used for the
embroidery work.

Huck toweling could be used with
this pattern.

77

# EYEGLASS (spectacle) CASES AND SEWING BASKET

*The eyeglass case with the fish design is embroidered with Swistraw (Raffine) on a coarse, loosely woven fabric.*

The case with the fish motif is a new type of the kind of eyeglass case that allows glasses to slide in and out. The case with the embroidered squares is the familiar type. The size of the case you make will be determined by the size of the glasses.

The eyeglass case with the fish motif is made of tapestry canvas embroidery with Swistraw (raffine). Make it in a size to fit your glasses. It is made in one piece. Make the side pieces to match, as shown in the illustration.

Stitch the design, using the pattern below, done with staggered stitches. At the transitions between the front and side piece, stitch an additional row as shown at the top of page 80. Embroider the bottom piece separately. It is five stitches wide and length matches the width of the case.

*Procedure.* Turn the embroidered canvas back at top edge and sew an edging stitch over two threads as shown in the drawing below. Press the work on the wrong side. Attach ⅜-inch wide cardboard pieces or corset stays to the side pieces with long cross-stitches. This insert will serve to protect the glasses.

Sew the lining in place along the top inside edge of the case.

*Fish design pattern.*

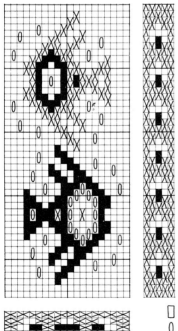

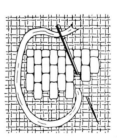

*staggered stitches*

*sewing the top edge*

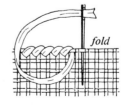

*fold*

▯ - *natural*
0 - *light brown*
X - *rust*
∎ - *brown*

79

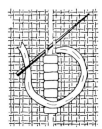

*Sewing together.*

Leave a thread hanging so you can sew the sides and bottom later.

Sew the embroidered case together at the side and bottom, using the stitch illustrated on the left.

Hand sew the rest of the lining piece and tuck it back into the finished case.

### Eyeglass (spectacle) case: type 2

Use the same embroidery pattern as was used for the handbag on page 38.

MATERIALS:
1 piece monk's cloth (castle erin), or coarse hessian 4″ × 22¾″.
Pearl cotton #8, two colors.
1 piece cardboard 2¾″ × 5½″.
1 piece thin foam rubber approximately 2¾″ × 10¼″.

*Procedure.* Overcast the raw edges and find the middle of the material in each direction. Mark it. Start the embroidery from this middle point and stitch a pattern piece four squares by two squares (using the pattern on page 39) for each side.
Press the embroidery on the wrong side. Place the right sides together and sew the side seams as shown in the drawing. The unembroidered portion should have the seams indented a fraction of an inch more than the seams on the embroidered part, as it forms the lining.

Turn the pieces right side out and insert cardboard on one side and foam rubber on both sides. Then sew the raw edges together. Stuff the lining down inside the case. Press the upper edge. The case is ready to use.

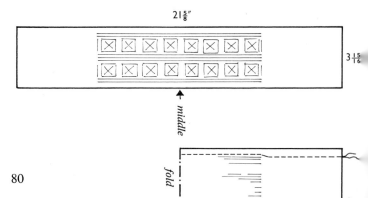

*Cutting pattern for eyeglass case. Type 2.*

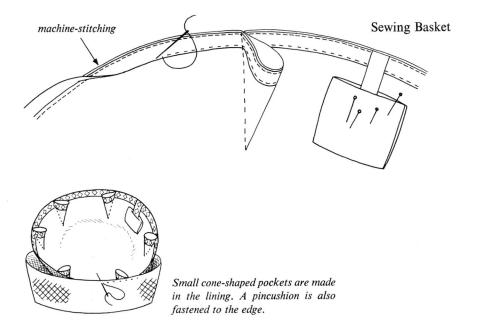

*machine-stitching*

*Small cone-shaped pockets are made in the lining. A pincushion is also fastened to the edge.*

## Sewing basket

Any round basket can be used to make the little sewing basket shown in the photograph. Or you can make your own basket. Directions for this one are given in *Weaving with Cane and Reed* by Grete Krøncke (Van Nostrand Reinhold, 1968).

*Procedure.* Begin by measuring the inside of the basket. Measure from the top edge down the side, across the bottom, and back up to the opposite side. Use this measurement as a diameter and cut a circle this size, plus a seam allowance.

*A handmade sewing basket is out-fitted with a lining that provides little pockets for sewing needs.*

Edge the circle of material all the way around with a binding. We used a decorative seam binding for this one. Stitch it on by machine, turn it, and hem in place. Bias tape is best for this purpose as it will lie flat on a curve.

Make six cone-shaped pockets by stitching the fabric as illustrated. The pockets can be in various sizes. A small one would be nice for a thimble, and larger ones for embroidery scissors and tape. Plan ahead, though, so when you have made all the pockets, the piece will fit the basket top. It's nice to sew a little pincushion to the lining piece too.

Attach the lining to the basket with invisible stitches.

81

# DECORATIVE HANGINGS

Many kinds of fabric and designs are suitable for decorative hangings. The one shown below on the left is blue tulle with snowflakes cut from paper and attached with iron-on pelon (moycel). A strip of iron-on pelon (moycel) is used for a border. If you hang the blue tulle piece against a window, it becomes almost invisible and you see only the dancing snowflakes. The one on the right is

*Decorative hangings are fun to make and can be most imaginative. Thin ones can be hung up in the windows for a striking effect. Others are nice as wall hangings, especially if you cannot afford fine paintings. They offer another fine way to exhibit your handicraft talents.*

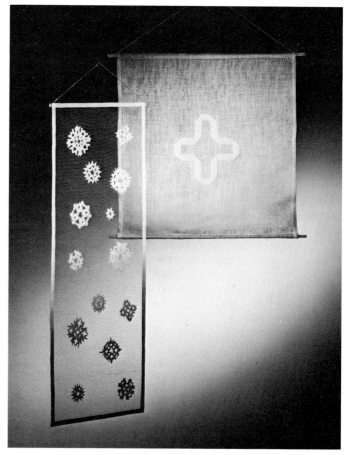

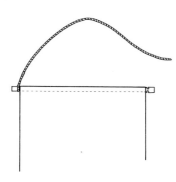

*Make notches in the dowel rod you use for your hanging to keep the cord from slipping off the ends.*

made of linen, hemstitched at the borders and with an appliqué design in the center.

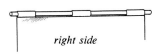

*right side*

## Bell pulls

Although bell pulls are rarely used as such in modern households, they are finding their way back as decorative motifs. They may be embroidered, handwoven, or textile printed. A very good-looking bell pull is shown in the cover of this book.

There are several methods for hanging these bell pulls. You can use expensive hardware, or you can use simple dowel rods or wooden rings. We show a few of the possibilities here. If you are planning a special hanging attachment for your bell pull, be sure to pick it out first before making the piece. You want everything to fit well and will need exact measurements for the attachments, such as perhaps a bell or ring hanging from the bottom of the pull.

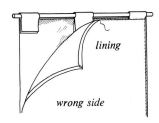

*lining*

*wrong side*

*For some bell pulls and wall hangings, this type of hanger is best. It keeps the top edge flat. Make the loops of matching material and hide the raw ends behind the lining.*

*Procedure.* Cut the fabric to be used to the desired length and double the width of the finished bell pull. In addition allow extra for a center seam.

Do the embroidery or other design work down the center of the fabric. When it is finished, press it on the wrong side. Press both edges back. Cut a piece of iron-on pelon or other stiffener that just fits the width of the bell pull. Press on the pelon (moycel) or catch stitch other stiffener-type fabric in place. Turn edges back and sew together with invisible stitches as shown.

Attach the hanger at the top and other hardware attachments, if desired, at the bottom.

Along the long sides you can sew on a thin cord, or you can sew along the edge as shown in the drawing at right. But this must be done before the assembly is done.

You may want to treat the back a different way. A separate strip of lining material can be hand-stitched over the interfaced bell pull. Both the edges of the front piece for the bell pull and the lining edges should be pressed back carefully in order to get straight lines and a careful fit.

Another simple method is to simply fold the front-piece edges back, and press them down. Then iron on pelon (moycel) over them. This only works on thin fabrics.

These bell pulls can be made in burlap (coarse hessian) and decorated with dried flowers. You can even make a long, narrow one with a deep pocket for dried flowers and interesting weeds.

*A decorative stitch can be made along the vertical sides of the bell pull. Or you can sew on a fancy cord.*

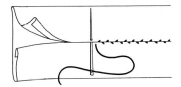

*This is the best way to handstitch the back seam together. Sew it carefully and right in the middle. Don't make it too tight.*

# FRAMING

*These pictures are framed with Mystic Tape (self-stick cotton tape). See text for details.*

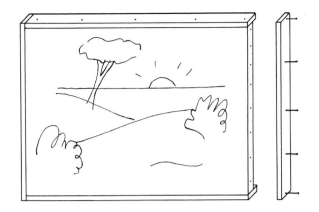

Framing

*Here's an easy way to frame a painting. Just nail the wooden molding to the canvas stretcher.*

It is expensive to have an expert make a frame, but it requires such exactness that many people do not want to try it themselves. The following is one that anyone can do.

MATERIALS:
Planed, untreated wood molding, $\frac{3}{8}''$ thick, and $\frac{3}{4}$–$1''$ wide.
Brads.

*Procedure.* The principle used in this method of framing is that the cut wooden moldings are nailed to the edge of the stretcher on which your canvas is stretched.

The diagram indicates the procedure. Cut the moldings to length, following the measurements of the frame. Remember to take the thickness of the molding into consideration on the two short end pieces. The cuts should be made in a miter box so that you can be sure of getting perpendicular and straight lines. Use a saw with very fine teeth (a hack saw or miter saw are suitable).

Nail the moldings to the edge of the canvas stretcher with brads ($\frac{7}{8}$ inch 17 gauge). Place the outermost brads on each molding piece a bit in from the end, because the wood can easily split if they are too close to the edge. Make sure the moldings fit flush in the corners when you nail them to the stretcher. Check to see that they protrude equally far out from the stretcher.

The best method is to nail the upper and lower horizontal moldings first, then mark and cut the vertical moldings. Attach two eye screws to the stretcher, equally distant from the outer edge. Attach picture-hanging wire for hanging the picture.

To keep the picture from shifting on the wall, glue a small piece of foam rubber on the back at the two lower corners.

85

**Quick-and-easy frame**

With Mystic Tape (self-stick cotton tape or carpet tape) and glass you can frame your handicrafts, children's first drawings, and the like, in an easy and inexpensive way.

Cut the picture with straight clean edges and right-angled corners. Cut a piece of white or colored pasteboard in the same size, or larger, to make an edge all the way around the picture. Get a piece of glass at the glaziers in the same size as the pasteboard piece.

Place the picture on top of the pasteboard and center it exactly. Place the glass on top and put small pieces of cellophane Scotch tape (Sellotape) here and there along the edge to keep everything in position. Make the actual frame of Mystik Tape (cotton tape). The width of the tape depends on the size of the picture, glass, and pasteboard back. You want enough to get a secure job. In most cases, ⅜ to ¾ inch width is fine.

Begin at one corner and start putting the Mystic Tape (cotton tape) on in such a way that the part visible on the front of the frame is equal all the way around. If you have trouble getting it even, mark the line with a grease pencil or china marker, which you can remove from the glass later.

It is easiest to do one side at a time. You could go all the way around, but it is hard to make trim corners that way. The first method has the advantage of being able to get more professional-looking corners by cutting the tape on the diagonal.

Pictures framed this way can be hung by attaching ready-made picture hangers to the back, or by gluing on string with ends frayed. When the glue has dried, the ends should be further secured with tape.


**Matted picture frame**

The procedure is the same as described above, except here you add a pasteboard matting sheet in which you have cut out a rectangular area for the picture. The mat serves as a border for the picture. The cuts must be cleanly made and the corners must be sharp right angles.

The easiest way is to draw lines on the board with a soft pencil. Use a drafting triangle to get lines straight and corners squared. Check your lines to make sure they are parallel, equidistant from the edges, and that the diagonals of the rectangle are the same. Otherwise your hole will be crooked.

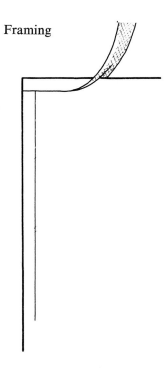

Framing

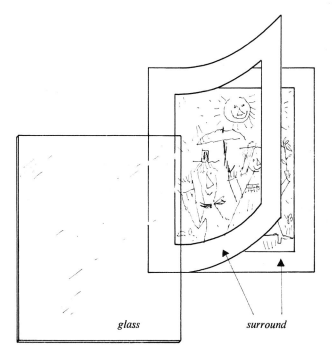

*glass*          *surround*

*A matted frame gives the picture a
little air space. It is assembled as
shown here. Mystik Tape (self-stick
cotton tape) is used for this simple
frame.*

When you are ready to cut, place the mat board on a heavy piece
of cardboard, or better still a wooden cutting board, and tape the
corners down so it won't slip. Use a utility knife or X-acto knife
(Stanley knife) for cutting and a steel ruler as a guide. Place the
ruler on the side of the frame that is to be used for the mat. It is
best to cut all the way through the first time, because repeated cuts
make the edges ragged and uneven.

Take plenty of time in marking and cutting. Errors become
magnified in the finished product. Besides, mat board is not cheap,
so you do not want to waste any.

**Gluing on cardboard**

It may be useful to glue pictures, clippings, recipes, tables, and the like on a piece of cardboard. To do this is the cheapest possible framing job.

You might use a thin wood trim for the edges. A 45-degree angled corner looks best on this trim, and you can even cut this very thin wood stripping with heavy duty scissors.

If you are gluing on cardboard, you must remember to glue a support on the back, otherwise the cardboard will warp. To prevent this, glue a plain piece of strong paper on the back of your cardboard.

Wallpaper paste or cellulose paste works fine for this job. You must weight it down with some books, or the like, while it is drying.

You can protect the picture with a layer of Saran Wrap, or spray it with a plastic preservative coating.

**Wooden picture frames**

Lumber yards and art stores have a large selection of planed wooden moldings in all kinds of shapes that can be used for picture frames. Ordinary frame moldings are difficult for beginners to handle, so a very simple method is given here. It does produce satisfactory results, nonetheless. Use the wooden molding that has a profile with a groove as shown in the diagrams. You can probably get these moldings in various sizes. They are usually available only in pine.

Use a hard fiberboard for backing the picture. This can be cut to size at the lumber yard. The sheet must be cut with straight edges and right-angled corners. You place the picture on the smooth surface of the fiberboard. The back is rough.

Cut the molding with a fine-tooth saw. Since the corners must be joined at a 45-degree angle, use a miter box with guides for the saw. You can buy these at most hardware stores.

Calculate the size of your frame piece according to the size you have cut the fiberboard. Measure the length of the molding pieces along the groove that the fiberboard fits into. Be very, very accurate. The diagonal cut on the molding must come exactly at the corner of the fiberboard.

When you have cut the four molding pieces, join them around the fiberboard. Position the two longest pieces first. Push the fiberboard into the groove in the molding and apply some epoxy glue

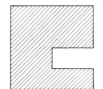

*Pictures mounted on a piece of chipboard or masonite may be framed with grooved moldings. At right is a section drawing of a grooved molding. The narrow part faces out. At left, the drawing shows how the corners are cut at a 45-degree angle.*

to the diagonal cuts at the ends. Put some glue on the diagonal ends of the short molding pieces and fit them into position. Align everything for the last time. Make sure the corner joints are tight—they will be if you cut them accurately.

While the glue is drying, tighten the frame with strings tied around it as shown in the drawing. Put a piece of folded paper or cardboard under the string so it won't mark the soft wood frame.

When the glue has dried, secure the corner joints with two very thin brads in each corner. To avoid splitting the wood, don't put the brads too close to the edge.

Screw two eye screws on the back of the frame moldings for the string or wire.

This method is very useful, but its practicality depends on finding a molding with a groove that fits the thickness of the fiberboard.

Sometimes you can find moldings with two grooves. Then you can use one groove for a piece of glass in front of the picture. Be very careful in driving the corner brads for this frame. You don't want to break the glass. It is a good idea to nail a triangle of plywood over the corners, in the back, to make the joint firm. Glue these triangles in place just before you start to hammer in the brads.

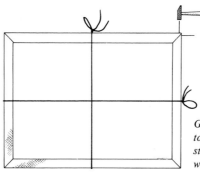

*Glue the four mitered corners together with hobby glue. Use strong string to hold the pieces together while the glue is drying.*

# MOUNTING PRESSED FLOWERS

The square lampshade shown is easy to make. (For instructions on lampshade making see pages 53–58.)

You will need 10-inch wide white synthetic parchment, one set square wire lampshade frames. Raffia. Pressed flowers. Hobby glue and cellulose lacquer.

*Procedure.* Frames are available at hobby shops. You can use lampshade parchment instead of synthetic parchment, but it changes color with use.

Measure the circumference of the frame and transfer this measurement to the parchment. Add $\frac{3}{8}$ inch for side seams. (If your frames are $6\frac{3}{8}$ inches on the sides, the circumference will be about $25\frac{1}{8}$ inches. Add $\frac{3}{8}$ inch to this and the measurement will be $25\frac{1}{2}$ inches. Figure the height the same way. This model is $9\frac{1}{2}$ inches high.

Mark the pattern with a soft pencil. Draw the lines all the way around and be sure they are at right angles in the corners. Use a drafting triangle and straightedge. Check to see that your corners are square and check the diagonals of the square in both directions to see if they are equal. If not, the shade will be crooked.

Cut the shade along the pencil lines.

Mark holes for lacing the shade to the frame and use a punch to make the holes. The holes should be small and placed about $\frac{3}{8}$ inch apart. Don't trust your eye for cutting these holes. You must mark the position with a ruler. Cut through a piece of cardboard or leather to cushion the punch. This makes the holes come out with a cleaner edge.

Put the two short sides together, and hold them in place with paper clips. Cut the holes through both thicknesses at once. The holes here should also be $\frac{3}{8}$ inch apart.

Lace the edges together with raffia as shown at right. Lace the shade to the top and bottom of the frame. When you have done this, make sharp folds exactly at the three corners (see photograph).

The lampshade is now ready for decoration.

*It is fun to use pressed, dried flowers as decorations on things you use daily. They remind you of happy times when you gathered them. Here a lampshade, tea canister, and trivet are all decorated with pressed flowers.*

Mounting Pressed Flowers

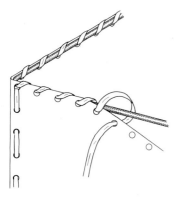

*This is the way to sew the lampshade together and to the frame. Note that the side seams make a sharp corner.*

Cut a piece of paper to fit one of the sides of the lampshade, about $6\frac{3}{8} \times 9\frac{1}{2}$ inches. Arrange your dried flowers on this to form an attractive layout.

When you are happy with the arrangement, sketch it on the paper and move the flowers one by one onto a newspaper, wrong side up. Apply glue and smooth it carefully with your finger. Move the glue-coated flowers cautiously over to the correct position on the lampshade, right sides up. Smooth into place.

Work from the top of your design down. In this way you will succeed in keeping the stems covered with the lower leaves. As you position the flowers, press them down on the shade material, using a soft lint-free cloth. It doesn't matter if you squeeze out some glue at the sides, since the white glue dries as clear as glass.

If you find a flower with too little glue, lift it and apply additional glue. Be careful with the glue, Avoid messing. Keep it free of hair, dust, and lint particles. They show up terribly.

After you have decorated all four sides of the shade and the glue is dry, lacquer the shade with diluted cellulose lacquer or clear cellulose lacquer. Use a soft brush. It is a good idea to apply two coats of lacquer, but make sure the first coat is completely dry before applying the second. Clear lacquer in an aerosol or a spray gun can make the job easy. The frame should have a mechanism for mounting the hanging socket.

## Trivet

Use a $6 \times 6$-inch piece of plywood. Decorate with pressed flowers glued on just as was done for the lampshade. Finish with a heat-resistant clear plastic laquer. Ask your local store manager about the newest and best laquers for this purpose.

## Tea canister

Use a metal tea canister. Clean it well with emery cloth and fine steel wool. Cover with white paint that adheres to metal. (Consult your paint dealer. Also purchase appropriate lacquer for the final coat. The two must be compatible.)

When the paint is bone dry, put a second coat of white paint on one side. Let the paint set a bit and while it is still tacky, press the flowers carefully into the paint. Let the decorated side dry, then repeat the process on the other sides. When all the paint is bone dry, lacquer the entire can.

92

This process takes a great deal of dexterity. You may prefer the glue method used for the lampshade and trivet.

## How to press flowers

You can find pretty leaves and flowers suitable for pressing just about the whole year around. When you are out hunting for suitable plants, it is a good idea to take along a plastic bag to carry them home in. This will prevent them from drying out on the trip home. Or you can take along an old book, and press the flowers as soon as you pick them. Then, when you get home, put something heavy on the book, or squeeze it into the bookshelf.

You can also press flowers between pages of newspaper. Cut the newspaper into four parts. Make a pile consisting of two pieces of newspaper, then flowers, then two pieces of newspaper, flowers, etc., ending with the newspaper. Then apply pressure to the pile. Use heavy books or bricks. Don't make the pile too thick.

Blue flowers, such as cornflowers or bluebells, need special treatment. They will lose their color completely, or partially, if you press them according to the above newspaper method. If you want to preserve the blue color you must put them in the newspaper and press with a lukewarm iron *first*. Then the blue colour will last through several years of exposure to sunlight.

After the iron treatment, press the flowers in the usual way.

Pressed flowers can be kept for years, so you might as well make an extra supply and have it available for your craft projects.

# INDEX